SAMIRA
IZADI PAGE

Who Is My
Neighbor?

CHURCH
PUBLISHING
INCORPORATED

A little
book of
guidance

Church Publishing
19 East 34th Street
New York, NY 10016
www.churchpublishing.org

Cover design by Jennifer Kopec, 2 Pug Design
Typeset by Denise Hoff

A record of this book is available from the Library of Congress.

ISBN-13: 9781640652149 (pbk.)
ISBN-13: 9781640652156 (ebook)

Printed in Canada

Contents

Introduction

When I was asked to write on the topic of "Who Is My Neighbor?", I was humbled by the offer and intrigued by the question. On the surface, it is a simple question. With careful consideration, it becomes a profound question with enormous consequences for each of us personally and for our world in general.

Depending on our cultural backgrounds, political persuasions, social settings, and religious frameworks, the question "Who is my neighbor?" can evoke a range of opinions and principles. Someone raised and living on a farm in an interior state in America has a far different view of neighbor than someone who lives in a high-rise apartment building in New York City. A well-traveled person is much more likely to welcome a new neighbor than a closed family who has limited interaction with people outside of their clan.

Whatever the influences, the answer to the question can be as varied as the people you ask. Some define neighbor as the person or family on either side of their home. Others may consider a neighbor as anyone in their suburban housing development. Still others may identify a neighbor through selective criteria such as age, interest, or ethnicity. There are also those for whom the question of neighbor has been given little to no attention at all.

Our world has been fundamentally changed by technological advances. Places and people once far away are brought close through the internet, social media, and e-mail. YouTube has caused broadcasters to re-strategize their programming and distribution services because the youngest generation of adults consume media in a completely different way than their parents. The grossly expensive international phone call has been replaced by a free video app on a smart phone. Most major cities across the world are now saturated with flight options; people can connect around the world with a few clicks on a website. And yet, the largest contributor to the question "Who is my neighbor?" is the massive migration of people.

According to the United Nations High Commissioner for Refugees, war, persecution, economic collapse, famine, political unrest, and natural disasters have combined to force more than 68.5 million people to flee their homes. It is the largest migration in human history. Whether it is refugees fleeing war zones, persecuted Christians seeking safety, or asylum seekers who have escaped political unrest, our neighborhoods are changing. And, with each new family we are forced to consider the question that is as old as the very first family: "Who is my neighbor?"

Since we live in a time marked by the largest migration of people, the question becomes, "How will the Church respond?" Put another way, "What does our God call us to do?" The time to respond is now and it is limited, both because of our available years of ministry service as well as the season of opportunity. This is the time for the Church to engage, with greater clarity and conviction than ever, those whom God is appointing as our neighbors. From tiny rural congregations to metroplexes saturated with megachurches, Christians must pray what the Psalmist prayed in Psalm 90:12, "Teach us to count our days that we may gain a wise heart." No other organization, individual, or system of beliefs has been so uniquely called and equipped by God to answer in practical and spiritual ways, "Who is my neighbor?"

In Genesis 4:9, Cain asked God, "Am I my brother's keeper?"

With that one question, Cain revealed a thousand words about his sinful heart. His cavalier manner has followed humanity through the ages and is with us today. Every time a Christian demonstrates apathy or disregards the sufferings of a neighbor whom God has placed within their ability to help, they point back to Cain's sarcastic question.

I am a former refugee who mobilizes churches to serve refugees. I also serve a refugee and immigrant congregation. I write on this topic from my own experiences and the experiences of people I serve—American-born Americans as well as refugees and immigrants. As a theologian, ministry leader, and someone whose life has been forever impacted by neighborliness, I know firsthand the importance of clarity in answering the question "Who is my neighbor?"

A lack of Biblical understanding about immigrants and refugees has turned simple discussions into intense debates, divided families, determined political elections, and led to the polarization of several Western nations, including America. Without a Biblical foundation to the question of what it means to be a neighbor, refugees suffer in camps or find themselves alone trying to eke out a living, even in the richest nation in history.

The terms *immigrant* and *refugee* have almost become dirty words in the public sector. My husband and I have a few Facebook friends who privately encourage us in ministering to refugees, but never comment or like anything we post related to the families we serve. The most docile personalities can be stirred to a fever pitch when pulled into political discussions about refugees and immigrants. However, long before immigrants and refugees became a political hot potato, the Sovereign of the universe had preordained where they would live and the lengths of time they would live there as seen in Acts 17:26–28:

> From one ancestor he made all nations to inhabit the whole earth, and he allotted the times of their existence and the boundaries of the places where they would live, so that they would search for God and perhaps grope for him and find him—though indeed he is not far from each one of us. For "In him we live and move and have our being"; as even some of your own poets have said, "For we too are his offspring."

This little book is designed to infuse biblical truth with righteousness for everyday Christian living so that we not only know who our neighbor is, but how to love our neighbor as our self. This book is for every Christian whose desire is to courageously connect to God's mission and purpose of being the witness of Christ to their neighbor.

1 ■ *Setting the Tone*

My Neighborhood

My husband is from a small town in Louisiana. He is in his mid-fifties. He has fond memories of the tight-knit community of family, friends, and neighbors. There are other memories that are not so pleasant. His very small town did not have a diverse population. He recalls knowing of only one Hispanic family and an Indian family that owned a convenience store. Other than those two families, the town was black and white—even the cemeteries.

When he began his kindergarten year, schools in his town were still segregated. About halfway through the term, desegregation finally reached his school system. He shared with me how scared he was as a little boy hearing his older brothers and sisters recall the racial fights that occurred nearly daily at their junior and senior high schools. Although the signs of "colored" and "white" had been taken down at restaurants and department stores, no one dared cross those invisible barriers.

One of his most frightening experiences happened around age four. A downpour came as he, his father, and his mother were almost home after shopping in a city about forty minutes away. His father pulled the car into a church parking lot close to their neighborhood to wait out the storm. There was no sign out front, but it was understood that it was a "whites only" church. My husband recalled how terrified he was of his father being hurt or put in jail for parking at that church. He fixated on the church doors, hoping no one would come out.

Part of his parents' driving lessons for him and his siblings was "the talk" that they were never to drive through certain neighborhoods, even if it was the shortest route to school or to the grocery store. That kind of counsel did not come from overzealous, misinformed parents, but from their experiences of living in a racially divided town.

My husband shared a story his dad told him about a night that as a child, his family slept in their cornfield. Word had spread that a white man had been shot and it was rumored that a black man had killed him. Law enforcement was going through the rural black neighborhoods collecting their guns. My husband's grandfather was so fearful of the anger toward blacks that he took his family and fled their home to spend the night in their cornfield, hoping the rage would have subsided by the next day. Even though everyone was born in America, my father-in-law was a World War II veteran, and his father was respected in his community as a faithful deacon who physically helped build the black church, their family was not treated as part of the neighborhood. By God's grace, my husband did not internalize those horrible experiences to the degree that they damaged his view of God or the mission of the Church.

What kind of neighborhood did you grow up in? What are your first memories of neighbors? Were you the kind of person who would reach out to the neighbors? I confess, although I am very comfortable with public speaking, I am overwhelmingly an introvert. I lived in a neighborhood for about thirteen years and did not know anyone except an older lady who lived to the left of my house. That neighborhood to me was more of a collection of houses than a community of people who had at least a moderate concern about one another. Unfortunately, it never felt like a real neighborhood.

It is an entirely different experience in our current neighborhood. We love it! It is one of the most diverse neighborhoods in our area of the city. We affectionately call it the Texas version of the United Nations. Although I am still an introvert, there is something that draws me out of my cocoon. I have come to know more people in the short time that we have been here than any other place I have lived. What my husband and I sensed shortly after moving in was the atmosphere of neighborly concern and oneness of purpose. As people walk their dogs, they greet us or even stop to talk when we are working in our yard. Because of that introduction into our neighborhood, we feel safe and welcomed. That warm welcome has given us a sense of responsibility to extend that same welcoming spirit to those new families moving into our neighborhood.

In Matthew 22:38–40 we read, "This is the greatest and first commandment. And a second is like it: 'You shall love your neighbor as yourself.' On these two commandments hang all the law and the prophets." Luke 10:27–28, gives us deeper insight:

> He answered, "You shall love the Lord your God with all your heart, and with all your soul, and with all your strength, and with all your mind; and your neighbor as yourself." And he said to him, "You have given the right answer; do this, and you will live."

It is fascinating to look at the two side by side. Together they teach us not only that loving God and our neighbor are God's commandments, but also that they are matters of life and death for *us*, not for the neighbor!

Be Ye Holy, Neighbor

When we think of a holy person, we tend to think of people such as the apostles and prophets—Mother Teresa or Dr. Martin Luther King Jr.—but the Bible tells us that you and I are not only to be holy, but we *are* holy. It is God who has made us holy by the work of the Spirit through Christ. Now, the holiness that has been credited to us is also the holiness that is to be made visible to the world around us through our words and actions. Being a good neighbor is one of the biggest and brightest demonstrations of holiness.

The command to love our neighbor is not something that Jesus offered as a new tradition. This commandment is found in Leviticus 19:18. A broader explanation is found in Leviticus 17–27, a passage that scholars call the "Holiness Code." These verses explain how the people of God ought to conduct their lives in such a way that they align with the holiness of God. Leviticus 19:2 provides the reason: "You shall be holy, for I the LORD your God am holy." In this portion of the scripture, God constantly reminds the Israelites that the reason they are to be holy is because of who God is: "I am the Lord." In light of Jesus's sacrifice on the Cross, understanding the connection between who God is and "love your neighbor" becomes a powerful expression of "holiness." Ephesians 4:14 and the need to imitate Christ finds a new significance considering this background.

Someone may be challenged to equate loving our neighbor to living in God's holiness. We know from the scripture that, apart from God, we are not holy nor can we make ourselves holy by acts of righteousness. The Bible tells us that no one is holy (1 Samuel 2:2); "there is no one who does good, no, not one" (Psalm

14:3); "there is no one on earth so righteous" (Ecclesiastes 7:20); nor is there anyone who does not sin (1 Kings 8:46, James 3:2, 1 John 1:8). We know that only God can make us holy, which allows God to dwell with us. "And in him you too are being built together to become a dwelling in which God lives by his Spirit" (Ephesians 2:22).

When Leviticus 19:18 tells us, "Love your neighbor . . . I am the Lord," we see how loving our neighbor is an extension of God's holiness into the world through us. In other words, if we have a saving faith that authentically transforms us, our desire to love our neighbor will be as natural as breathing. Notice I did not suggest it will also be easy. If you are a non-smoker dining on a restaurant patio where several people around you are smoking, you will find it difficult to breathe normally, but the natural desire to breathe is still there. As Christians, it will not always be a simple and comfortable effort to love our neighbor, but the spirit of God will produce within us, like breathing, a desire to find ways to do it.

Consider the myriad of conflicts, dissensions, bickering, and splits that happen daily within the Church across denominations. The frequently prevailing attitudes and actions of the Western church are more in line with cultural individualism, personal faith, and narcissistic Christianity, which make "me" the center of the faith rather than the person of Jesus Christ and God's commandments. As we make a close examination of the Ten Commandments, we find the commandments to love God and to love our neighbor are the fulfillment of the Law. The first three Commandments are about God. The rest is about the neighbor. They instruct us to do or not do things to other people. Even the Commandment to keep the Sabbath provides rest not only for the individual, but for the entire family, including servants and animals. In light of the slavery and oppression the Israelites themselves experienced in Egypt, Sabbath is a way of lessening the burden and bringing the rest of justice into the lives of the servants (Deuteronomy 5:12–15).

It seems like we cannot call ourselves faithful to Jesus and to the Bible unless we love our neighbor. Loving our neighbor is not a condition of our salvation, but it is a proof because "faith [without] works, is dead" (James 2:17).

A Vivid Picture

If you serve at a church in any capacity—leadership team, worship team, choir, administration, or staff—you know how easily and quickly schedules fill up. There is always something that is demanding our attention. Our personal lives are not much different. There are the daily household chores such as cleaning, cooking, laundry, shopping, and paying the bills. Outside of the home, there is work, getting the kids to soccer or cheerleader practice, and small group meetings. Just like that, our lives are packed with activities.

If you were to examine your weekly schedule, how much time would you find is given completely to growing in personal holiness as shared above? If you are in full-time ministry, how much of your day or week do you have built into your schedule for intentionally developing in personal holiness? What amount of time is spent in the relational ministry of being a neighbor?

In Luke 10, the Parable of the Good Samaritan provides the quintessential biblical text on the topic of neighborliness. Here, the expert in the law stands up and asks how he can inherit eternal life. The question is a significant one. He is not asking for an answer to a procedural question or a small functional matter. He is asking about eternal life, life that will last forever. It was only natural, and rather urgent, that the expert wanted to know who his neighbor was.

Before further examination of this text, we need to know the context so that we can accurately grasp the expectations of the writer. Trying to understand who our neighbor is can be a fruitless effort if we have no idea why we should know them. Mister Rogers, the Presbyterian minister who educated and entertained children for decades, sang a simple but profound song to children every day for more than forty years, asking them, "Won't you be my neighbor?" Have you ever lived in a community where his lyrics were true?

We learn about the good people serving our neighborhoods. However, when Jesus taught about neighbors, that was not exactly what he had in mind. It is good to be neighborly to the people who are in the house across from ours, and to those who are just like us. They will likely return the kindness with warmth and goodwill. But, if an occasional exchange of pleasantries is the extent of our neighborliness, we do not understand the biblical idea of being a neighbor. We need to drastically change our expectations if we are to have standards of neighborliness that align with the will of God.

What Would You Do?

Luke 10 has an interesting structure. Immediately before this parable of the Good Samaritan, we read about the sending of the seventy-two. You may think the two are unrelated, but they are intimately connected.

Jesus sent out the seventy-two to different towns ahead of his arrival to prepare the way, much like John the Baptist did. When you meet different people at work, at the store, or on the bus, have you ever considered yourself as the one who prepares the way of the Lord? If you became more deeply aware of this reality, how would it change the way you talk to others, conduct business, dress, spend money, or live your life? We must remember that we are the only Bible many people ever read and the only church they encounter.

In 10:3, Jesus said that he sends them out as lambs among wolves. These followers of Jesus were armed only with the Good News of the coming Kingdom of God, and were to heal those who could be vicious, dangerous, unwelcoming, ungrateful, unscrupulous, deceptive, and unthankful for the help offered them. Why would Jesus send them among the wolves? Can the so-called "wolves" receive healing and the message of God? Are they deserving of healing?

Who do you perceive as "wolves"—dangerous individuals, groups, or people with whom you would have a difficult time sharing God's healing? Like the seventy-two, Jesus sends us out into the world, into our neighborhoods, our places of work, immigrant and refugee communities, children's soccer communities, and ballet performances regardless of the conditions these situations present.

It is interesting that the warning in verses 13–15 does not have to do with the response of individuals. The warnings have to do with towns or communities that are welcoming or un-welcoming.

Verse 5 of Luke 10 deals with another revealing aspect—peace. In the context of individuals, peace is the quality of a person's character that connects with the same quality in another. This, again, is prior to sharing any message. Can a "wolf" be a person of peace? Can there be people of peace among groups that we may perceive as "wolves"? Is anyone beyond redemption and healing? Examine your heart and how you perceive different individuals, races, and nationalities. Then, consider what Jesus would tell you about reaching them with his healing and love.

A Vulnerable Kingdom

Verse 9 has another lesson: "Heal the sick who are there and tell them, 'The kingdom of God has come near to you (NIV).'" Our assumptions about what the Kingdom of God is and how neighborliness works are challenged by Jesus. We live in an individualistic culture where life is about "me" and doing what I want to do the way I want to do it. Other individuals and groups are free to do their own thing as long as they respect and do not challenge me. We are usually private about our affairs and how we handle them.

Gospel neighborliness is the opposite of our cultural ways. Yes, Jesus is counter-cultural. Gospel neighborliness puts us in a place of vulnerability. It means that our family in Christ who genuinely cares for us will ask loving, but sometimes probing questions. They will concern themselves with what is best for us. Neighborliness opens us up to being changed as well as being used by God to bring change into others' lives. Healing the sick means that our sickness can be exposed as we serve others and are being served, unless we think that we are fully perfected and have no sin or sickness in us.

Neighborliness is a process in which God confronts our prejudices, fears, shames, weaknesses, and insecurities—known and unknown. It is a process of discovery and learning. Are we, who are still being healed and still sin, willing to be vulnerable so that God can use us, and in the process, heal us?

My Neighbor Is (Dignity and Choice)

Jesus tells his disciples that they will go to places where many people will not be loving or welcoming, but he sends them anyway. Jesus teaches us just as he taught the seventy-two that we are to respect the dignity of others and allow them to make choices. The stern warnings of verses 13–14 are additional examples of how to treat others with dignity and respect. We are to speak the truth in love, rather than treat lightly matters with serious consequences or coddle someone to merely appease them. Speaking the truth in love is treating others with dignity.

I am a Muslim-background believer and it is my passion to share with others my story of God's healing and transformation. When I was in seminary, I met with the person in charge of evangelism for a church. As we were discussing Muslims, she said that she never talked about her faith or God's work in her life with Muslims because she wanted to respect their belief. I believe her intentions were good. But, as someone with many family members who are Muslim, I could not help but interpret the comment as offensive to the dignity of Muslims as people created in God's image. What I heard was that she was making the decision for her Muslim friends that they did not need to hear her story of God's work. I heard that her Muslim friends did not have the ability to discern, to be led by God and to make a choice; she made the decision for them. What I heard was a colonialist attitude that said, "I know better than you and I choose for you," rather than sharing from her heart within the context of genuine friendship and love, then allowing her Muslim friends to choose. Jesus calls us to treat others with respect and dignity even when they may not receive what God has for them.

This principle is true, not only in regard to spiritual matters but also practical ones. Inside my ministry, Gateway of Grace, we serve refugees from various countries and different religious backgrounds. We see spiritual realities within communities and individuals whom we serve. As people with dignity, they choose whether or how deeply to engage with our staff and volunteers. Perhaps the most important lesson about our neighbor is that our neighbor is the person or persons with dignity who are free to make choices, and sometimes that choice means rejecting us, our help, and yes, even our love. We are not their savior. And we are not the Holy Spirit who brings convictions of the heart to matters of truth. This is a difficult truth to contend with as, most often, those of us with compassionate hearts want to fix everyone we meet. Sometimes our neighbors simply do not want to be fixed.

Early in my ministry with refugees, I was overeager to tell our refugee friends everything I knew about how to do things here in the United States. Little by little, I learned that some of them wanted to experience and learn about life in America on their own terms. It often costs them deeply, but it is their choice. It breaks my heart to see our refugee families in trouble. I know that if they had just listened to what I shared with them, they would not be going through such difficult times. But I have come to accept that my "neighbor" is with all their gifts, graces, good-heartedness, and sins, as any other human being. I must honor that.

Several years ago, I met a persecuted Christian family from Iran. Their circumstances forced them to flee to Turkey, where they lived for a few years waiting on their refugee cases to be processed. The family had a son who suffered from diabetes. I met the family as soon as they arrived in the United States. As it turned out, we were from the same hometown in Iran, so it was a very sweet meeting. Gateway of Grace began serving the family and the nineteen-year-old son. We helped him get a job at a restaurant. He had to be at work very early in the morning. His commute was about ninety minutes, changing a few trains in the dark hours of the morning. I was concerned about him. Although he was a smart person and a hard worker, he had limited English and even less understanding about what it took to thrive in the United States. We raised money through the ministry and purchased a car for him. He was over-joyed. We asked him to continue at his job that had potential for promotion, and to keep preparing to attend college. The car was a tool that empowered him to do both at the same time.

After a few months, he met other young Iranians who influenced him in unproductive ways. He quit his job, borrowed money to buy and sell cars, lost money on a car, and quit college. Six years later, he does not have a stable job and has not finished college. Early on, we met with him and counseled him, but we realized that, regardless of the wisdom we shared, he was going to make his own decisions about life. It was painful to watch him inflict wound after wound upon his life. We continue to pray for him, and are committed to providing the same wise counsel should he want it.

A Loaded Response

Jesus's parable provides a profound response to the lawyer's question, "Who is my neighbor?" Jesus was intentional about saying, "A man was going down from Jericho." He didn't identify whether he was an Israelite, a good person, a family man, an adulterer, religiously observant, or an unbeliever. The man could have been anyone for the sake of neighborliness, it did not matter. He then identified those passing by the man, which included a Levite, a priest, and a Samaritan. Religiously, the Levite and the priest were held in the highest regard and the Samaritan was the lowest; the Samaritan was the outcast. The Levite and the priest claimed righteousness, were faithful to religious practices, prayed publicly, performed the sacrificial ceremonies, and attended synagogue regularly. Jesus finished telling the parable and asked. "Which of these three do you think was a neighbor to the man who fell into the hands of robbers?"

Notice the response of the lawyer. He was not able to bring himself to say that the Samaritan was the neighbor, a demonstration of the disregard the lawyer had for the Samaritan. Instead he said, "The one who showed him mercy" (Luke 10:37). Jesus told the lawyer to go and do as the Samaritan had done, which was a slap in the face of the religious authorities who considered themselves holy and righteous. Jesus said it was better to be a Samaritan who was a neighbor than a priest or a Levite who was not. Can you imagine how shocking these words of Jesus must have been? Jesus turned things upside down.

No More Scapegoating

Looking for a scapegoat is a natural part of our sinful psychological makeup. As a matter of fact, psychologists have determined that almost as soon as children can express themselves verbally, they know how to pass the blame. The behavior follows us into adulthood. The motivations for scapegoating are basically the same for adults as they for children: we do not want to feel the guilt of our sin, acknowledge responsibility, or deal with consequences of actions or inactions. Neither is scapegoating a contemporary problem only. From the first family to our family, we find people who choose the convenience of passing on the blame. Of course, what we call scapegoating has biblical roots that at its core had quite a different origin from how it is used in societies today. Let us examine Leviticus 16:7–10 (NIV):

> Then he is to take the two goats and present them before the LORD at the entrance to the tent of meeting. He is to cast lots for the two goats—one lot for the LORD and the other for the scapegoat. Aaron shall bring the goat whose lot falls to the LORD and sacrifice it for a sin offering. But the goat chosen by lot as the scapegoat shall be presented alive before the LORD to be used for making atonement by sending it into the wilderness as a scapegoat.

The last part of the passage about sending the goat into the wilderness is particularly significant because we, in our daily lives, go through the same process. While God's scapegoat had a holy purpose, ours is selfish.

We usually do not think about how our scapegoating impacts others. Instead of asking how he could serve the neighbor, the lawyer asked Jesus what qualifications one should have in order to be considered a neighbor. In other words, the lawyer's question was intended to find reasons that would disqualify people from being served. Jesus, knowing the heart of the lawyer and the motive for his question, pointed out that neighborliness was not about who "those people" were, but who we are. As Christians, our lives must be marked by attitudes and actions that demonstrate the presence of God. We know and embrace the command to love God, but when loving God moves into the realm of loving our neighbor, we become like the lawyer in the story and look for disqualifying reasons to care for someone.

I am a frequent speaker at churches, where I share my testimony of coming to faith and creating a ministry that mobilizes the Church to reach refugees. I am often given a question-and-answer time at the end. It is rare to finish a question-and-answer session without at least one or two questions that are similar to the question the lawyer asked Jesus, aiming to disqualify someone as a neighbor. Remember, Jesus sets no qualification for who our neighbor is. Anyone can be a neighbor. God provides the example of how to love our neighbor. "But God demonstrates his own love for us in this: While we were still sinners, Christ died for us" (Romans 5:8).

Take a moment for self-examination. Do you ever or often try to qualify people in order to be neighborly to them? In what ways do you find a scapegoat when it comes to loving your neighbor? How do you demonstrate love for the neighbor who simply can be a challenge to love?

2 ▪ *What Is Love?*

By now, we have established that the Bible provides empirical evidence that loving God and loving our neighbor are inextricably connected. What needs deeper exploration is the meaning of love. With all due respect to legendary and award-winning singer Tina Turner, her song "What's Love Got to Do with It?" was wrong on so many levels. Love is definitely not a second-hand emotion. Love does not break hearts; it mends them. And love is certainly not an old-fashioned notion. But Ms. Turner is not the only one getting it wrong when it comes to understanding and using the word *love*. The Church also shares in the guilt.

Saying "I love you" has become one of the many Christian expressions we are expected to share with one another. We say it to people with no real evidence or demonstration that we really love them. Other than a two-minute interaction in the atrium or a greeting in Sunday school, what evidence is there, in most cases, that we love our brothers and sisters in Christ or that they love us? When we ask about their week or their family, many of us do not ask with the desire to hear about how much their child is messing up in college or how they are struggling with putting her parents in a nursing home. We care, but just not to a point of altering our day. At best, we ask "How are you?" as a conversation filler so that we feel good about acknowledging their presence and to show all is good between us.

I will answer Tina Turner's question, "What's love got to do with it?" Everything. If any group of people on earth should know the meaning of love, it is Christians. After all, our God is Love. Love is the ultimate expression of our faith. And we were called into God's family by love and commissioned to demonstrate love unconditionally. Claiming to love God without loving my neighbor is no more possible than drinking a glass of water without getting my lips wet. In Greek, the language of the New Testament, there are six words for love:

- *Philia* (φιλία): affectionate regard and friendship, usually "between equals."
- *Eros* (ἔρως): passion or love expressed physically; from which we get our word erotic.
- *Agape* (ἀγάπη): the love of God for humans and of humans for God. Agape is used by Christians to express the unconditional love of God for his *children*. Thomas Aquinas explained it as, "To will what is good of another person."[1]
- *Storge* (στοργή): tender affection, particularly of parents and children.
- *Pragma* (πράγμα): a model of love as two people may demonstrate during a lengthy marriage or partnership.
- *Philautia* (φιλαυτία): self-love.

The kind of love we ought to have for our neighbor is agape. Agape love is of and from God. It centers on goodwill for another person and is based on God's moral preference. Agape love is seen by what it does. However, this love does not mean allowing people to do whatever they want. It is about God's preference. In simple terms, the question is always, what does God want? To love (agape) means to want what God wants for another person. But it goes further. Agape love is the moral essence of God. It is the same word used when we read, "God is love." Agape love has the power to generate or regenerate (1 John 4:8).

What does God's love generate? What are God's purposes? I can best answer those questions through a simple practice I use. I interpret everything in the Bible in light of the gospels. Everything in scripture finds its meaning based on the eternal purposes of God who is Agape. Let's explore this further through a few verses from the Gospel of John.

John 3:13 tells us, "No one has ascended into heaven except the one who descended from heaven, the Son of Man." It means no one fully knows God's will and purposes or what God wants except Jesus. John 3:16 unfolds the truth of the ages: "For God so loved the world that he gave his only Son, so that everyone who believes in him may not perish but may have eternal life." The word for *love* here is *agape*. What is generated by this love is eternal life. This agape is not just for one person or group, not just for the Church or for Christians, but for the world. Consider for a moment the magnitude of this proclamation. No other religion uses this depth of love. At the heart of the one true God is a heavenly parental care for every man, woman, girl, and boy for all times and that they should live with God forever.

John 3:17 continues: "God did not send the Son into the world to condemn the world, but in order that the world might be saved through him." Here we see God's purposes for sending his son into the world. God desires that all people would be saved, not condemned. God's love is not a Western creation perpetrated upon the world. It is an incomprehensible expression of the Creator for all creation so that every person in every nation should know God and God's love for them. As ambassadors of God, we are obligated to give this message to people across the five continents, and especially to those whose access to this message of agape love has been hindered or forbidden. We know that the character of God does not allow partiality. His love is no less for people in Syria, Saudi Arabia, Pakistan, Iran, India, the Philippines, Venezuela, Cuba, or the Congo than it is for people in Las Vegas or Detroit.

Agape is a missional love. This is the kind of love the Apostle Paul calls for in 1 Corinthians 13. He says if we do not have this regenerating, active, moving, life-giving love for the entire world, we do not have agape love, and, in that, we have nothing and are nothing useful for the Kingdom of God. Remember, we have established that agape is the moral essence of God. And when we have this love, we have the presence of God through the Holy Spirit at work through us.

That is why in the same chapter of the book of John, Jesus tells us that unless we are born of water and the Spirit, we cannot enter the Kingdom of God. It is the Holy Spirit in us that enables us and changes us into having agape love and moves us into inspired actions. This is the kind of love that causes our illegitimate divisions to cease. This kind of love provides a witness that we are indeed followers of Jesus Christ. "By this everyone will know that you are my disciples, if you have love (agape) for one another" (John 13:35). Whenever there is a discussion about missions, it is intentionally or unintentionally a discussion about God's agape love for the world.

So, we have within us different kinds of love: love for a spouse, children, extended family, friends, the good of humanity, and for self. But do we have agape love, which is the moral essence of God? The good news about agape love is that God is already pouring it into the world, for all people, and all we need to do is connect with what God is doing.

I met an Iranian woman who came to the United States with her husband in 2017. Her husband was an engineer in Iran. The woman and I were talking about Jesus when she began to share with me this fascinating story about her mother. Her father had gone bankrupt in Iran and the family lost everything. They were forced to live with relatives in Tehran. For various reasons, that arrangement did not last long and the family was asked to leave. They had nowhere to go.

One morning, the mother went walking to shield her family from her brokenness. As she was walking and crying, she came upon a church in Tehran. She sat down on the steps in front and prayed to Jesus; she then passed out from the anguish. When she woke up, an elderly man was calling her and asking her what was wrong. She soon discovered that the man was the father of her childhood friend who had died about a year prior. The woman shared her family's story. The elderly man told her to walk with him. It turned out to be a miraculous journey. He took her to a vacant apartment that he owned and said, "See, no worries. You and your family can live here." The family immediately moved into the apartment.

But the story does not end there. Sometime later, the elderly man bought the family a very nice home. This woman's story was a modern-day Good Samaritan parable. As her daughter who now lives in the United States shares her mother's testimony, she is fully persuaded that Jesus orchestrated this miracle and all the events that led to this amazing blessing for her family. She is now seeking Christ and wants to know more about him as a result of those events. This is one example of God's agape love that is continually at work in all places and its extension throughout generations.

Agape love is not about being a nice person, or sharing pleasantries in a coffee shop, or making a point to always smile at the grocery store cashier. It is surrendering to God a blank check from our life, allowing God to fill in whatever amount of love a situation needs, then joyfully signing it with "Yes, Lord." Through those moments when we say "Yes, Lord," we agree to become the people who love the neighbor to the glory of God.

There are three core components to agape love: being aware and concerned about others, asking what God wants for others, and taking actions to bring about God's purposes in those situations.

In light of what we have covered about agape love, do you feel you demonstrate it on a regular basis? Specifically, what are you doing daily, weekly, or even once a month to allow God's agape love to flow through you to people next door, down the street, on your job, to a family on the other side of town, or to people from other countries and religions? Do hinderances remain, such as prejudices, misinformation, unfounded fears, or even unconfessed dislike for people out of your comfort zone? If any of these exist, I ask you to agree with God that they produce a hinderance to people seeing in you a clear representation of Jesus Christ. Pray in faith that God will help to remove those obstacles and gain unhindered access to your heart.

Imagine if someone just purchased a lot of expensive furniture: a beautiful sofa and loveseat, a large 4K television, a dining room set, and things for the bedroom—but they did not have a house for the furniture. Instead, all of the furniture just rode around in the back of a truck for weeks and weeks. While the person owns the furniture, none of it is getting its proper use because it was not created to ride around in the back of a truck. It was created to be used in the context of a home. So it is with all of the other meanings of love. Without a comprehensive understanding of agape love, the other five meanings of love can never find their truest expressions.

Every secular music category with songs about love will invariably connect love to a feeling. The biggest problem with our feelings is they change, depending on the circumstances. Our feelings change because they are attached to our emotions. And our emotions are influenced by a variety of biological, psychological, and other external factors.

Thanks be to God that agape love is not based on emotions and feelings. Agape love originates in the spiritual realm grounded in the character of God, is undeterred by circumstances, and its essence is to bring the goodness of God to its recipients in practical ways. That is why the Christian can love their enemies and bless those who persecute them.

Finally, there are three action items to agape love.

1. Ask the question, "What does God want for others?"
2. Care for others even when it is difficult.
3. Be a part of fulfilling God's plan for others.

Our Spiritual EKG

America has a heart problem. According to the Centers for Disease Control and Prevention, about 610,000 people die each year from heart disease. That is one in four deaths. Every year about 735,000 people in America have heart attacks.[2] America's heart problem is staggering. Thankfully, advances in healthcare are helping more people discover heart disease much sooner.

One of the most impressive healthcare advances in heart health is the electrocardiogram, more commonly called the EKG/ECG. The technology allows healthcare professionals to check for signs of heart disease, monitor electric activity of the heart, and check for any abnormalities, among other issues. A series of electrodes are attached to various parts of the body, and data is collected in a matter of seconds. It is simply fascinating technology.

What is true about the physical hearts of Americans is true of many spiritual hearts in the Church. The Church has a heart problem. The prophet Jeremiah said, "The heart is deceitful above all things, and desperately sick; who can understand it?" (Jeremiah 17:9 ESV). While this is not a condition brought on by a bad diet or inactivity, it is a result that can largely be blamed on feeding our souls the spiritual junk of the world and not being actively involved in real Kingdom work.

One of the major contributors to poor spiritual heart health is the unguarded manner in which we allow the world's values to form our spiritual views. For several years, the media has had a feeding frenzy over refugee and immigrant stories, and the majority of coverage has been from a polarizing political perspective. You are either in this camp or the other, this political party or the other. Please know that I have absolutely no interest in taking a political position on these issues. My call, and more specifically the Church's call, is much deeper than temporal politics. God is after the hearts of people to affect positive systemic change in the conditions of our neighbors, and my hope is that God will always find us working there.

When I started my ministry of mobilizing churches to serve refugees years ago, about a third of church leaders I met with showed low levels of interest in partnering with us. Another third were more focused on fact-finding about refugees, seemingly wanting to be sold on why their church should get involved. The final third simply got it and were ready for their congregations to get involved in whatever way possible. I confess there were some discouraging days, but the call and commitment remained clear. I needed to stay the course, love my brothers and sisters, and speak the truth in love about this global crisis that was increasingly landing at the doors of American churches.

An interesting thing began to happen a couple of years in. As the immigrant and refugee rhetoric ratcheted up in America, more and more church leaders began to contact me. As we met, they talked about how ill-equipped they felt their church was in dealing with this growing world crisis. There were leaders who had never interacted with a refugee and certainly did not know how to relate to them or support them.

As a Muslim-background believer whose family members are persecuted Christians, I understand the feelings that are stirred in those opposed to immigrants and refugees. I have had lunch or coffee with many who needed to work through their fears and deep prejudices. I have tried to graciously answer what they asked during the question-and-answer sessions of my messages but were embarrassed to verbalize publicly. I eagerly have done so because I see myself as an instrument in the hands of God to heal the hearts of the people so that they can get on with the business of being neighbors to refugees. That is the task of any minister. It is not my place to judge the fears and prejudices of those who disagree with me, but to meet them where they are and show them what God is doing around them. As the anger toward immigrants and refugees has continued to fill the airwaves and social media, more Christian leaders have asked to meet with me. Meeting after meeting has led to sharing with church leadership teams and then their congregations. God has clearly been stirring in the hearts of the people. What a blessing it has been to see the spiritual growth of fellow Christians. Those who were once apathetic and fearful of refugees have become their advocates, defenders, and supporters.

Like any work of God, evil forces are not far away. That certainly has been the case for me and the ministry. While God was providing favor with many churches, organizations, businesses, and civic leaders, the enemy of our faith seems to have had tremendous influence over many other Christian leaders, some of whom I respected. There were social media posts from leaders that spewed vile anti-immigrant and refugee comments. Other prominent leaders sounded more like politicians than proclaimers of the gospel. I was more disappointed than angry. My disappointment stemmed primarily from knowing that these otherwise faithful leaders allowed their hearts to be hardened to God's work in and amongst refugees.

Meanwhile, the mainstream media was unwittingly portraying the worldwide immigrant and refugee crisis as though it was the first in history. That could not be further from the truth. While it is the largest in history, it is by no means the first time for a mass migration of people. During World War II, tens of millions across Europe fled their homes to escape the Nazi war machine. The rhetoric that surrounds immigrants and refugees today is much the same inflammatory speech that forced sixty million people to become refugees or displaced people in the 1930s and 40s. There are volumes of analysis and research analyzing what created the conditions across Europe that led to World War II. I suggest that long before it was a social, political, and even racial issue, it was a matter of the human heart that had been hardened and had become incapable of knowing what it meant to be a neighbor and to love a neighbor.

Peter Shulman, a historian and associate professor of history at Case Western Reserve University in Cleveland, Ohio, used data from a 1938 July issue of *Fortune* to demonstrate the attitudes toward European refugees. Many of those refugees were Jewish and trying to flee Hitler's genocide. According to the poll, 67.4 percent of Americans believed that the government should refuse entry to the Germans, Austrians, and other political refugees from Europe. On January 20, 1939, another poll on a proposal to bring ten thousand refugee children from Germany—most of whom were Jewish—to be taken care of in American homes, reflected a 61 percent "no" response. Shulman, reflecting on America's response to the Syrian refugee crisis and the response to the Jewish refugee crisis during WWII, adds, "But in terms of a heavily politicized, nativist response to a refugee crisis, we have been here before. And the example of Jewish refugees fleeing Europe in the late 30s is most poignant because we know how it ended."[3]

During World War II, a ship named the *St. Louis*, filled with Jewish refugees from Europe, tried to find refuge at America's shore. It was denied access, at which point it returned to Europe. The Nazis entrapped the Jewish refugees on board. This is one of America's darkest experiences with refugees. In the wake of World War II, the United States admitted over 250,000 displaced Europeans. In 1948, the first refugee legislation enacted by the United States Congress was the Displaced Persons Act.

Further laws helped the admission of people fleeing Communist regimes from countries such as Hungary, Poland, Yugoslavia, Korea, China, and Cuba. The majority of these refugees were assisted by private ethnic and religious organizations in the United States. In 1975, the United States resettled hundreds of thousands of Indochinese refugees through an ad hoc Refugee Task Force. The Congress passed the Refugee Act of 1980, which incorporated the United Nations High Commissioner for Refugees' definition of "refugee." But these acts were in the shadow of the above-mentioned public disapproval and hostile emotions.

Just as the Syrians are the face of refugees today, the Jews were the face of refugees during World War II. During that dark period in human history, the Church mostly remained silent across the world. Certainly, no systemic, powerful, or prophetic opposition took place. "Christians, in particular, became painfully aware of the ways in which the age-old 'teaching of contempt' toward Jews and Judaism had paved the way for the Nazi program of hatred, dehumanization, and genocide."[4]

Here is the point: the difficulty of loving our refugee and immigrant neighbor is not an issue of terrorism or Muslims, just as it was not about the Jews or Catholics. People strive to find a reason outside of themselves to justify their unjustifiable fears and hatred. Unfortunately, professing Christians are not insulated from this kind of reasoning because the root of the problem is spiritual. In Romans 7:22–23, St. Paul lays out his human condition and how it is diametrically opposed to the spirit of God within him.

> For I delight in the law of God in my inmost self, but I see in my members another law at war with the law of my mind, making me captive to the law of sin that dwells in my members. Wretched man that I am! Who will rescue me from this body of death?

Paul's battle with sin is our battle. No matter how sophisticated we have become, as a society in general or a church in particular, no one has completely escaped the corruption that is the flesh. And evil spiritual forces are constantly at work seeking to dismantle God's purposes for the Church and God's specific plans for our lives through any means necessary. God's plans for the Church are for it to be empowered by the Spirit to exalt Jesus Christ and his love in the world, and to bring glory to God. The task of God's people is to be thoroughly equipped for the work of being Christ's witnesses to the world, and to bring healing and hope to the wounded and the hurting. But strong forces of evil work relentlessly to prevent Christians from recognizing or engaging their Kingdom work of caring for their neighbor.

If God were to perform an EKG of your spiritual heart, what would God find? What about your church? More importantly, would you be willing to change attitudes and actions so that you can live a heart-healthy spiritual life?

The Nature of Obstacles to Loving Our Neighbor

The Wounds of the Church

"We believe in One, Holy, Universal, and Apostolic Church."[5]

When we recite the beautiful words from the Apostle's Creed, "We believe . . . ," we are making a declarative statement that frames every word in the sentences that follow. But how often do we give deep consideration to the words of our creed? I suggest that if more people in the Church truly pondered the rich history and meaning of those words, we would experience a dramatic change within the Church. If more Christians embraced the words "One, Holy, Universal, and Apostolic Church," the cancer of illegitimate divisions would show deep decline. Afterall, divisions within the Church are like kryptonite to Superman: it is the one sure way of weakening her power.

When the Church tolerates these unbiblical divisions, the results do not remain within the Church only, as many would like to believe. The negative effects are far reaching and the Church's family fights seem to be amplified among unbelievers who are often looking for a reason to justify their rejection of the Christian faith. When love for our fellow Christians is not great enough to overcome these divisions, we unintentionally shape the view of those outside the Church: "See, how can they talk about loving their neighbor when they can't even love one another?" What a horrible witness.

In 1 John 4:20, John holds back nothing in exposing the hypocrisy of some professing followers of Christ. "Whoever claims to love God yet hates a brother or sister is a liar. For whoever does not love their brother and sister, whom they have seen, cannot love God, whom they have not seen" (NIV). With some of the most politically incorrect language possible, John calls into question the salvation of any person who claims to belong to God yet does not love their own family. In the same spirit, how can someone claim devotion to God and deny their neighbor? Jesus said the law and the prophets hung on these two commandments: "'You shall love the Lord your God with all your heart, and with all your soul, and with all your mind.' This is the great and first commandment. And a second is like it: 'You shall love your neighbor as yourself'" (Matthew 22:37–39). Just like there are illegitimate divisions within the Church, there are also unsanctioned discriminations emanating from the hearts of some believers. When

Christians stifle the promptings of the Holy Spirit to be a neighbor to someone of a different race, religion, or nationaliy, they are denying the resurrection power of Jesus Christ to change hearts and heal wounds, both of themselves and their neighbor.

I am not of the mindset of some Christian leaders who blanketly condemn the idea of denominations. The scripture obviously does not commend or condemn denominations. What it does make unequivocally clear is that Jesus Christ has One Church which is his Body. In this Body, we are many members and members of one another. We are not a variety of gifts, talents, and abilities that assemble weekly to express ourselves. We are instead the Body of Christ, who is the head, and are to be completely submitted to his purposes in the unity of the Spirit. When illegitimate divisions are allowed to reign, they put on display a spiritual immaturity, and damage or even destroy our witness to the world. Consider the priestly prayer of Jesus in John 17:22–23 (ESV):

> "The glory that you have given me I have given to them,
> that they may be one even as we are one, I in them and
> you in me, that they may become perfectly one, so that
> the world may know that you sent me and loved them
> even as you loved me."

Illegitimate divisions in the Body of Christ also have an impact on evangelism. When arguments among Christian siblings are made public, unbelievers question the authenticity of our faith. After all, how can it be real if it does not unify its own followers? What unbeliever wants to hear a Christian talk about God loving them when racism, sexism, classism, and nationalism mark their faith?

N. T. Wright, New Testament scholar and retired Anglican Bishop of Durham in England, often reminds us in his lectures that unbelievers look at our fights and think to themselves, "Who wants to be a part of that bunch?" In my own ministry, Muslims often ask me what the difference is between this church and that church. I am quickly reminded that these very religious people take notice of our differences and attitudes toward each other.

Sin

Another obstacle to loving our neighbor is actually the ultimate hinderance to loving God and living a healthy Christian life. All of us are infected with the spiritual disease called Sin. There are many definitions, but at its core, sin can be defined as an offense against reason, truth, right conscience, and God. "It is a failure in genuine love for God and neighbor. It wounds the nature of [humankind] and injures human solidarity." Sin can be described as "an utterance, a deed, or a desire contrary to the eternal law." In action, "Sin sets itself against God's love for us and turns our hearts away from it. Sin can be distinguished according to its object, as can every human act; or according to the virtue it opposes, by excess or defect; or according to the commandment it violates."[6]

Ultimately, sin is a heart issue and a spiritual matter. There is no denying that sin and repentance are unpopular topics of discussion among many Christians today and are rarely in many churches and sermons. In some, sin has been reduced to a sort of disorder that can be fixed if only we get the right attitude or are able to love enough—a kind of sentimental approach. The truth from scripture is something quite different. Isaiah 64:6 defines

Sin as an infection, and Romans 3:23 defines it as something that no human being can avoid. In the words of Archbishop Desmond Tutu, Sin is "radical brokenness in the world." It is the outworking of evil, powers and principalities. Sin manifests itself in a variety of ways within the Church. I consider fears, prejudices, and hatred the three most common ways sin in the Church is expressed toward neighbors who are different from us.

The term *xenophobia* appeared regularly in the 2016 elections. Xenophobia is the dislike or fear of foreigners. Immigrants and refugees were hot button political topics that eventually became core issues on the campaign trail. One of the core positions for several candidates was the message that these people are unlike us, don't have our values, and many of them are simply bad actors. I was as shocked as I was disappointed when I moved through social media and saw many high-ranking professional friends and fellow church and ministry leaders espousing some very hurtful comments about immigrants and refugees. First, none of what I saw was based on facts. It was only conjecture. Second, their comments seemed to reflect the views of their candidate rather than the godly people I had come to know. And most importantly, I thought often about how taking such a view publicly would damage their abilities to be effective civic leaders and ministers of the gospel.

While some fears can serve us well, such as avoiding a poisonous snake, locking the car doors, or knowing when not to invest, most fears can be summed up as irrational responses. Living a fearful life is inconsistent with our Christian faith: "for God gave us a spirit not of fear but of power and love and self-control" (2 Peter 1:7 ESV). Jesus often told his followers, "Don't be afraid, believe God." It would be against the character of God to call us to love our neighbor while prompting us to fear those he has appointed for us to love.

Part of what gives xenophobia its stronghold in the minds of people are their prejudices. Prejudice is a preconceived opinion that is not based on reason or actual experience. It is to judge character without knowing its content.

What are we to do with sin that causes us not to love our neighbor? Ironically, the answer does not rest completely on those who are guilty of the sin. Sin is a powerful weapon in the arsenal of our enemy, the Devil. As a matter of fact, it is the atom that compromises every wrong that has or ever will be committed against God. For that reason, we need a power that is greater that the power of Sin. God has provided that power to us through the Holy Spirit. The essence of the Holy Spirit is indescribable power, purity, and righteousness. Defeating sin against our neighbor requires us to allow the Spirit of God to work into our lives the power to overcome the sin, to purify our hearts concerning our neighbor, and to act righteously toward them. The assurance we have is that God's Holy Spirit has one comprehensive purpose in our lives, revealing and convicting our hearts of sin so that we are in right relationship with God and our neighbor.

I shared earlier that the answer does not rest completely on those guilty of sin against a neighbor. The optimal word is *completely*. We still have a part in addressing sin. When the Holy Spirit reveals the sin, we must take action. Merely acknowledging sin does not remove it any more than seeing a stain on your shirt cleans it. Our acknowledgment must lead to an action that leads to removing the sin. We simply must confront the sin of not loving our neighbor, whether it is a personal sin in my heart or a public sin in the Church. As Edmund Burke, the Irish statesman, eloquently puts it, "The only thing necessary for the triumph of evil is for good men to do nothing." There is nothing more challenging and satisfying than allowing God to change us as he deems right to make us useful for the Kingdom work.

Powers and Principalities

What comes to mind when you read the phrase *powers and principalities*? Other than the King James version of the Bible and its related translations, you probably think of the word evil. The entertainment industries of the world have made billions from movies depicting evil, whether in dark, serious films, or silly comedic cartoon characters. In truth, there is nothing innocent about evil or the powers and principalities that perpetrate it. Powers and principalities are the unseen rulers and authorities of evil that permeate our world. They do not have an inexhaustible playbook of schemes in their efforts to oppose the work of God. Their evil plan largely hinges on distracting, disrupting, discouraging, and trying to dismantle the institution of the Church. Their strategy is quite simple: take every possible advantage of Sin and radical brokenness in the world to tempt the Church not to take seriously its mission in the world.

When we visit a church, we make a judgment about the experience. "It was a warm church." "It was a very cold church." "Everyone was extremely welcoming." Or, "I felt I didn't belong." The truth of the matter is, we did not meet everyone. We most likely met a few people in passing and formed an opinion based on extremely limited interactions with no real data. The generalization we made about the church is a reflection of what we believe the prevailing spirit among the congregation to be.

This was an attitude I was intentional about avoiding as I built the ministry of Gateway of Grace. In the early days of our refugee ministry, I met with a few church leaders who seemed determined to communicate to me in subtle but clear ways that they were not remotely interested in introducing their members to foreigners, especially from countries where American soldiers had been killed in war. After those very short meetings, I would return to my car and remind myself of what God says about those challenges. "For our struggle is not against flesh and blood, but against the rulers, against the authorities, against the powers of this dark world and against the spiritual forces of evil in the heavenly realms" (Ephesians 6:12 NIV). I had to remind myself that the church leader did not intentionally seek to harm the gospel. After all, no church leader starts the day with a desire to hinder the congregation's biblical mandate to love your neighbor as yourself. But like anyone, a church leader can succumb to the schemes of the devil, and in a moment of weakness rely on human reasoning, rather than allowing the Spirit to illuminate the work of God around him.

Scripture uses terms such as "prince of darkness" and "powers and principalities" to communicate a mysterious reality about the forces of evil that are a part of the invisible world. The Bible sometimes describes this as the "heavenly realm." Regardless of the terminology or whether it is an individual, group, or organization, the forces that seek to influence us are real and they have a myopic view of their purpose: render the Church powerless. Evil is rarely as it is depicted on television or in the movies. In other words, we likely cannot discern evil in a matter of seconds as with a movie character. In a movie, the character is often dressed in black, lurks in the background, and has a sinister look. That works well for the movie industry, but it is far from reality. The evil that is set against the Church and the Christian is unassuming, seemingly innocent, and often appears as a good thing.

Consider for a moment the toxic prosperity doctrine or the numerous cults that use the Bible to persuade people to leave their families and careers. While we know from scripture that the authorities of hell will not overthrow the Church, it does not mean that these forces cannot cause chaos, confusion, and destruction. If you are like me, you have seen far too many church splits, interdenominational fights, and complete closures of church buildings. In the heap of rubble from these fights and splits are the witness of the Church to the world and the proper formation of faith for many believers.

The Great Commission commands that we take the Good News of Jesus Christ to the ends of the earth. In the Cross of Christ, heaven and earth—God's realm and creation—were bridged. God became incarnate and the Holy Spirit descended. The Great Commission makes us all neighbors no matter where we are, even to the ends of the earth. But, the work of Satan is to divide and conquer the people of God for the ultimate prize of nullifying the indescribable work of the cross which is for the salvation of the WORLD.

Spiritual Apathy

There is no more insidious problem for the Church today than the highly infectious disease of spiritual apathy. This ever-increasing spiritual plague is consuming entire denominations. It is like an undetected, slow-growing cancer that is killing healthy cells in the body, making the whole body sick, weak, and facing death. Apathy is a lack of feelings, emotions, concern, or interest. What makes spiritual apathy so insidious is that it often attaches itself to at least a small measure of pride or unbelief. No sound-reasoning Christian consciously denies the core doctrines of the faith, the call to make disciples, or Jesus's command to love your neighbor as yourself. It is through false teachings and individualistic cultural upbringing that one fails to deem things that are not self-serving as parts and parcels of salvation. Many churches today would not dare make its congregation uncomfortable with a call to take the love of Christ to a nearby nursing home or to adopt an inner-city high school and become neighborly to underprivileged teens.

Another victim of spiritual apathy is the grace of God. Because our new covenant with God is based completely on God's immeasurable grace, our unguarded sinful nature can presume a grace without checks and balances.

I acknowledge that it can be difficult for even mature Christians to avoid such a pitfall when they are bombarded with messages that God loves them and wants their life to be happy, full, and problem-free, and that God's grace covers every wrong action or thought. Who can maintain a sober perspective on the Christian faith with such a monumental amount of sensationalized grace? However, even a modest glance at the Church will reveal that spiritual apathy is real and growing.

One of the clearest insights into what Jesus thinks about spiritual apathy is revealed in John's message to the Church of Laodicea.

> "I know your works: you are neither cold nor hot. Would that you were either cold or hot! So, because you are

lukewarm, and neither hot nor cold, I will spit you out of my mouth. For you say, I am rich, I have prospered, and I need nothing, not realizing that you are wretched, pitiable, poor, blind, and naked. I counsel you to buy from me gold refined by fire, so that you may be rich, and white garments so that you may clothe yourself and the shame of your nakedness may not be seen, and salve to anoint your eyes, so that you may see. Those whom I love, I reprove and discipline, so be zealous and repent." (Revelation 3:15–19 ESV)

The members of this church thought they were just fine with the Lord, not realizing that, in their current condition, Jesus wanted nothing to do with them. Among their ailments, Jesus pointed out they were blind. Scripture does not reveal to us the specific nature of their spiritual blindness. We know they did not see themselves accurately because they saw themselves as needing nothing. He told them to anoint their eyes so that they could see. And he told them to become zealous, or in other words, to have passion for the purposes of the Church rather than self. If the Church is to be cured from the invasive cancer of spiritual apathy, it must invite the Lord to purge every insidious sin.

Fears, Prejudices, and the Unknowing

I love the Church: the Body of Christ, God's people, everyday faithful Christians. It is truly a joy to serve Christians across denominations. Working across denominations has enriched my Christian journey in ways I would not have otherwise known. In my years of mobilizing the Church for refugee and immigrant ministry, I have met thousands of people and heard from hundreds of them about what they think and how they feel about our neighbors who are different than us. These folks are good people and most of the time have a genuine desire to learn more about what God is doing through my ministry. It is a blessing to see how the Holy Spirit is at work in them as they open themselves to new ways of thinking about Kingdom work. I always have in mind that I, too, must love my neighbors who are the Christians I meet every week. As a minister who is called to equip the saints for the work of ministry, loving my neighbors takes a special shape in the context of Church. With each interaction, I try to learn more about where sisters and brothers are and what the stumbling blocks to them are as they learn about loving their neighbors. What I have learned about their struggles can be put into three categories: fears, prejudices, and lack of knowledge.

Casting Out Fears

Fear is a complex emotion. Healthy fear keeps us safe because through it we learn to lock our doors and avoid risky behaviors. Unhealthy fear causes us to react in ways that are unnecessary, counterproductive, and most importantly, miss the will of God. That is what many Christians do when they are led by their fears rather than faith. More often than not, the adversary is steering our thoughts toward fear, the kind that does not acknowledge our loving and providential God. Considering the words of Paul, take heart for "in all these things we are more than conquerors through him who loved us. For I am convinced that neither death nor life, neither angels nor demons, neither the present nor the future, nor any powers, neither height nor depth, nor anything else in all creation, will be able to separate us from the love of God that is in Christ Jesus our Lord" (Romans 8:37–39 NIV) and the perfect love of Christ casts out all fears (1 John 4:18).

When the Lord gave me the vision to start Gateway of Grace Ministries, my husband, who at the time was the news director at a Christian radio station, was supportive but very fearful for my safety. In fairness to him, he had years of reporting on Christian persecution in Muslim countries. He understood the reality that converting to Christianity or any other religion was a crime in Shariah Law and punishable by death. Before meeting me, he had not known any Muslims from Muslim countries. His mindset about foreign-born Muslims was formed by the news he had reported. I kept reassuring him about my safety, but his heart was not at peace. He was, however, a prayerful and Spirit-filled man and knew the Lord was leading me into this ministry. At first, he came with me to visit refugees. He had a measure of alertness, but eventually he started feeling more comfortable. He has a very outgoing personality and a propensity to find what is common in our humanity. After a while, he would say things like, "When are we going to have Mohammad and his family over for dinner?" or "We need a plan to help this family."

What happened to my husband? The perfect love of God did not leave my husband alone and compelled him to obey God's command to love his neighbor. God's amazing love compelled my husband to ask the agape question, "What does God want for these refugee families?" As he listened more sensitively to what God was saying, his fears faded and his heart was freed to love his Muslim neighbors. Perfect love drove out my husband's fear, and my husband's heart toward Muslim refugees was transformed. My husband did not need to begin with feeling warm, fuzzy, and safe about serving Muslim refugees. He needed to obey what the Holy Spirit was revealing to him. Today, he has a remarkable ministry and reputation among our Muslim refugee families. At our major events that draw hundreds, he never sits, but interacts with as many refugees as possible and many of them seek him out.

Fear of Terrorism

The root word *terror* means fear. The goal of terrorism is to produce mass fear that ultimately leads to an abandonment of peace and freedom in a community or country. The single most frequently asked question I get from Christians is, "How can we know that Muslim refugees and immigrants are not really terrorists?" It is a legitimate question that deserves a comprehensive and thoughtful response for which, in fairness, this book does not allow sufficient time nor space. What I—as someone who has been through the vetting process—can share is that the United States government takes seriously the safety of its citizens and way of life, and the thoroughness in which it investigates each person wanting to come to this country should ease Americans' fears regarding refugees and immigrants. As a Muslim background believer, I appreciate the protections and freedoms I am afforded as an American citizen through the incomprehensively detailed work of federal, state, and local law enforcement officials. But the harsh reality of terrorism is that it is an equal opportunity employer.

The evil that gives birth to terrorism can be conceived in the mind of anyone who feels disenfranchised, marginalized, unaccepted, oppressed, and desperate for their perspective of justice.

While certain groups of people may garner a majority of media coverage and stereotypes, the brokenness that leads to terrorism does not belong to one group but is a sickness in the soul. As an example, mass shootings across the United States reached record highs in 2018 with 340. A mass shooting is defined when four or more people are shot. The overwhelming majority of 2018 mass shootings were by the hands of young white American males or American-born people.

For refugees, it is often terrorism, in the form of war or systematic persecution of a group, that causes them to flee. For example, years before Syrian refugees began arriving in the United States, they saw thousands of their fellow citizens killed at the orders of a horrendous dictator. Many of those who survived and managed to escape carried with them post-traumatic stress disorder, or PTSD. In their case, the fear of terrorism was real, and they have the psychological wounds to prove it. While the Bible does not specifically address fear of terrorism as it is known today, God's word is replete with admonitions not to live in fear, but to instead live in love.

Prejudies

What comes to mind when you see or hear the word "prejudice"? There are many variables that inform our thoughts and feelings about the word. Prejudice means to pre-judge. The actual definition is a preconceived opinion that is not based on reason or actual experience. Prejudice is an invasive and pervasive sin that at its root is a symptom of a spiritually diseased heart. It is invasive because we cannot totally insulate ourselves from the sinful influences of our fallen world. Whether we were taught certain prejudices as a child or adopted those preconceived beliefs later in life, we have always had exposure to the sinfulness of prejudices.

Prejudice is pervasive because it is allowed to spread like wildfire across our society when people are unwilling to confront it quickly, openly, and unapologetically. Prejudice expresses itself in attitudes and actions that are unjustifiably discriminatory. This spiritual deformity transcends human classifications, geography, and history. As much as our nation has advanced in race, gender, and socioeconomic relations, the tentacles of prejudice still have a firm grip on our society. And more than fifty years after the height of the Civil Rights Movement, racial prejudice seems to still have a stronghold on America. Scholar Ched Myers asserts that "Tension between fantasies of racial supremacy and realities of racial diversity remains one of the supreme challenges facing the United States, and thus our churches, today."[7]

Of all the challenges the church in America faces today, none is quite so self-inflicted as prejudice, expressing itself through unbiblical biases that deride the dignity of others for the sake of elevating oneself. Prejudices are often rooted in the idea that certain people are worth less or are less capable than others.

My husband is African-American born and raised in Louisiana. Whenever we meet someone new and he mentions that he is from there, people are most often surprised by his lack of accent and say, "You don't sound like you are from Louisiana." Being an African-American, he gets stereotyped in a variety of ways. People are usually further shocked at his high level of articulation and clarity of thought, as though that should not be the case. From our days of dating until now, I am astounded by some of the things I have seen him experience simply because of his race. I, on the other hand, am regularly stereotyped as a Mexican because of the way I look. I usually go along with it since I speak Spanish.

We all categorize people as a way of organizing life: adults, children, single, married, student, good, bad. Each category has certain characteristics, attributes, and liabilities. Negative stereotypes make up the basis for prejudices. Negative stereotypes about women, for example, lead to the formation of prejudices that make it more difficult for women to obtain positions of leadership. And when women attain those positions, the struggle is not over. There is overwhelming evidence through various studies and research that prove women are paid less than their white male counterparts.

Many of our neighbors in the United States are Muslims. A growing number of new refugees and immigrants in the United States are Muslims. The prejudices that hinder Americans from loving our Muslim neighbors can be attributed to the rise of Islamophobia. Peter Skerry, a professor of political science at Boston College, compares the experience of Muslims in America as a minority group to the experience of Catholics in the 1920s.[8] Current dominant anti-Islamic sentiments are much like the anti-papal sentiments of the early twentieth century. Muslims are portrayed as intruders and are associated with various vices. Andrea Elliott, a reporter on Islam in America for *The New York Times*, told the *Harvard Political Review*, "In the aftermath of 9/11, Islam and terrorism became almost synonymous in the media."[9]

This book is not about Islam, but about our roles and responsibilities, as Christians, toward all our neighbors. Loving our neighbor enables us to learn to see the person behind issues. This is a major step toward healing and reconciliation, which we, as Christians, are commanded to do. As a volunteer of Gateway of Grace reflected, "My opinion of Muslims and refugees hasn't changed much over the last three years of serving them. My opinions of the religion of

Islam is not much different. However, I am more able to distinguish the individual from their religion."

Of the many problems prejudice has in common with fear, one is that they both hold a person back from sharing the love of Christ with his or her neighbor, the very reason God has left the believer on earth. Once the soul has been severely scared by prejudices, the refugee, the immigrant, the poor, and the marginalized neighbor are not seen as worthy to hear the Good News or experience the practical love of Christ. Either knowingly or unknowingly, the person with prejudices in the heart overrules God on who should hear about the Savior and experience blessings that God intended to flow from that Christian.

When a Christian suppresses the promptings of the Holy Spirit through a heart of prejudice and chooses not to love his or her neighbor, it is an attack on God's unconditional love. The spiritual plague of prejudice is magnified when it is based on the externals of race, ethnicity, or origin because it dishonors and disallows the creative genius of God.

Media and Formation of Prejudice

How much consideration do you give to where you get your information about other races, religions, or places of origin? What are the primary sources that help form your opinion about people outside of your group? The overwhelming majority of Americans with whom I have spoken have never been to the home of a Muslim refugee or recent immigrant. Nor have they developed a friendship with a foreigner. Many refugees and immigrants from the Middle East, not unlike Hispanics and South American peoples, face the experience of living like rejected outsiders in American society.

Those most vocal with anti-Muslim and anti-refugee sentiments usually have no personal relationships with these people, but their opinions are formed by the media. The influence of mass media in forming both individual and societal attitudes is evidenced by the amount of investment in advertisement.

Did you know that the United States spends more on advertising than any other nation? "In 2016, more than $190 billion were spent in advertising in the United States. This figure is more than double the amount spent in advertising in China, the second largest ad market in the world."[10] That is an incredible amount of money. It is expected to reach the $207 billion mark in 2019. Television has been the biggest advertising medium in the United States in the last few years, but is expected to eventually fall behind digital. TV advertising revenue is forecast to grow from $73 billion in 2016 to around $82 billion in 2020.[11]

Most of us think that if we see something on TV or read it on the internet, it must be true. I experience this in my own field of theology. I constantly warn our refugee congregation about this, as it is nearly impossible for a lay Christian to discern and decipher all that is online. From lazy theology to bad theology, the internet and TV are full of misleading and, often, false claims. In addition to media, there is also the problem of systemic ways that certain organizations try to shape us.

One of the drawbacks of the influence of the media is that it draws our attention to certain aspects while ignoring others, and therefore it sets new standards. This approach to news skews reality, and it creates a perception of events that may not be in line with the Christian responsibility to love our neighbor. An example of this is the reports on the day of the Paris terror attacks a few years ago. On the same day that Paris had a series of terrorist attacks, similar attacks took place in Beirut. The attacks in Beirut left forty dead. Because the major networks chose to focus on the terror in Paris, we did not have the opportunity to hear about the attacks in Beirut. The result of the media's choice was that Beirut did not have the chance to receive the world's condolences, prayers, and financial support. Christ's love was not shown toward the people of Beirut because, we, Christians, didn't learn about it.

As David Paletz, the author of *Media Power Politics*, points out, "Reporters bring to any story attitudes, knowledge, and understandings which have a significant influence on the stories they produce. These attitudes, understandings, and knowledge must be recognized and included in any explanation of how the media create their special reality."[12] The problem lies where the public, many of whom are Christians, does not readily recognize this bias. The public takes the "special reality" of the media as the whole truth. This is a major problem for the mission of the Church in general and fulfilling the commandment to love our neighbor in particular. While we Christians attend church once or twice a week, we watch television news and read online political and social articles every day. We get far more of what shapes our views on refugees and immigrants from Fox News or CNN than from faithfully examining the scriptures, seeking wise counsel, and praying.

When we lack firsthand knowledge or do not have personal experience about an issue, we are by default dependent on our under-informed to uninformed opinions on such critical issues. However, when we were baptized into Christ, that supernatural act also baptized us into his truth about the world and how his followers are to live in it. The two usually don't match.

Even pastors can become negatively influenced by false or misleading media reports about refugees and immigrants. They can easily and quickly forget that they are shepherds and that God's call on their leadership is to guide Christ's flock in God's ways, not that of the world. So, how do we overcome the powerful negative influences of media? First, Christians need to recognize and remember that media, whether broadcast, print, or social, is driven largely by ratings, which translate into revenue. While there are very serious journalists, producers, writers, and assignment editors, they are a part of a much larger organization that cannot exist without revenue. Christians need to remind themselves that while we are in the world, the worldly ways are not to be in us. There must be a predetermined commitment for the Christian that biblical truth will always shape his or her worldview. Standing with truth and for the heart of God will most often put the Christian at odds with the world's views, and in some cases in opposition to the views of family and friends. What is popular, even among some Christian leaders, may not be the true story on refugees and immigrants. Be prayerful about allowing political commentaries to take over your social media platforms. You never know how God may be using your presence on them to attract those not yet Christian but open. One inflammatory, emotionally driven, and divisive post can do years of damage.

The Christian must be willing to allow the Holy Spirit to break the bonds of prejudices and biases so that the Spirit is free to guide the believer through the maze of mainstream and social media reports on refugees and immigrants.

The Unknowing

Unknowing and fear are related. We are usually fearful, or at least cautious, about things that we don't know. I am intentional about not using the term ignorance here. Unknowing is a lack of maturity in knowledge and is distinct from simple ignorance. Unknowing is when limited, biased, or otherwise partial knowledge and misinformation shape our perceptions. For our purpose, it is rooted in learning through a certain political or social lens without empathetically considering other lenses. The Bible is very emphatic about the need to gain knowledge and earn the ability to discern between truth and falsehood:

> The heart of the discerning acquires knowledge, for the ears of the wise seek it out. (Proverbs 18:15 NIV)

> Teach me knowledge and good judgment, for I trust your commands. (Psalm 119:66 NIV)

> Get wisdom, get understanding; do not forget my words or turn away from them. (Proverbs 4:5 NIV)

By knowledge, I don't mean getting information from one news source (which as we established is inevitably biased) and form an opinion. Knowledge is much more.

For the Christian, knowledge, first and foremost, is from God. It is a matter of using the whole counsel of God, interpreted by the ultimate revelation of God in the Gospels. I once heard a nationally known pastor from the Dallas area use a verse from the Book of Esther in an effort to justify his political stance against refugees and immigrants. More than anything, I was deeply heartbroken that he used his position of spiritual authority to possibly turn some from compassion to hatred toward refugees and immigrants. The unfortunate reality is that scripture has been distorted through the ages to justify horrendous injustices and inhumanities such as oppression, classism, and certainly slavery. It is among our greatest stewardships as Christians to handle the Word of God with accuracy and honor because we will be held accountable for how we use it.

Another major source of knowledge is relationships. We see Jesus in relationship with people throughout the Gospels. Jesus was not a guru who meditated in a cave then sent instructions through his followers on how people should live. His life touched the lives of many. Jesus dined, conversed, listened, and laughed with broken people. His ministry was in proximity to those he and his disciples served. He left us a beautiful example of how our lives are to touch the least and the lost. How can we gain a more accurate understanding about who they are, and what their hopes and dreams are, if our lives never touch? Apart from drawing near to the marginalized and the stranger, we will never discover the depths of our common humanity.

Imagine for a moment how fulfilling life would be for you and me if we applied these biblical principles to people who are different from us. Take a moment to envision that life. We immediately see the difference between where we are and where we should be. When it comes to our refugee neighbors, preconceived notions of Islam and Muslim cultures foment into fear and hatred, creating deep spiritual wounds. The world watched as reports came in about the 2015 Paris terror attacks. We sympathized with the pain and tragic loss of innocent lives. Although thousands of miles away, many of us in the United States suffered wounds from those attacks. Not physical wounds, of course. Many were wounded in their souls, feeling that humanity was not getting better, but worse. The evil one behind those attacks is the same one who will use terror to evoke fear and hatred in us, if we allow it. The result is Kingdom work that is hindered or left undone.

Since unknowing is based on a lack of knowledge that helps shape biases and perceptions, it has real-world implications. Such was the case for a woman who partners with Gateway of Grace Ministries. What is special about her situation is she leads the mission and outreach at an Episcopal church in the Dallas-Fort Worth area. She explains,

> Before working with refugees, I had limited experience with refugees or with Muslims, in particular. While I have plenty of family and friends from other countries, I don't know many people from the Middle East, and I only have two Muslim friends. My husband is from Haiti, though, and while he wasn't a refugee, I think my perspective of refugees is perhaps more informed than many people, at least in some limited way, because of our connection to Haiti. Before serving at Gateway of Grace, the stereotype of a refugee that I had in my head was of "boat people" from Haiti, trying desperately to make it to the Florida shores. You see, even those of us who have exposure to international relationships, don't know much about certain nationalities, races, or religions.

This woman is a dear friend who faithfully serves our refugees families. Exposure to refugee families helped her to gain the knowledge to make informed decisions and choices about building relationships with our communities. Through knowledge gained, her heart began to overflow with compassion, even more than before, for our families, and she became an even bigger advocate for our ministry.

Unknowing can also lead to scary thoughts. When people are not knowledgeable about a particularly sensitive subject, the uninquisitive response is to presume an answer. I experience this, firsthand, when I speak at churches. Although I make clear that I sincerely welcome each and every question about my life, Islam, and refugee ministry, it still can be difficult for those in the audience to ask the tough questions, publicly. But it is rare that someone won't come to me after the question-and-answer time to ask the really tough questions. One very popular question I get is, "Do refugees and immigrants make any contributions to society, or are they simply burdens imposed on us?" In this case, I share data from a study that was done in Australia with a similar refugee population as the United States. Australia is one of the major destinations for refugees.

A 2010 executive summary by the Refugee Council of Australia reveals hopeful results. "The 740,000 refugees and humanitarian migrants settled by Australia since Federation have had a profound impact on the nation's social, cultural, and economic life." The report finds that refugees "have found success in every field of endeavor, including the arts, sports, media, science, research, business, and civic and community life." Additionally:

> Migration and the intake of refugees can diversify and enhance the skill level of the population, increase economies of scale, and foster innovation and flexibility. [A great] illustration of this was evident in the 2000 Business Review Weekly's annual "Rich 200" list

which showed that five of Australia's eight billionaires were people whose families had originally come to the country as refugees.[13]

In the United States, a 2013 report on the Economic Impact of Refugees in the Cleveland area that was prepared for Refugee Services Collaborative of Greater Cleveland, confirms the results from the report in Australia. The study in the United States also finds that refugees are thriving in Cleveland and are at or above average compared to national norms in socioeconomic integration. Additionally, refugee activities in the Cleveland area in 2012 created about $1.8 million in tax revenue for the state of Ohio. In addition, the cities and other municipalities in Cuyahoga County are estimated to have received close to $600,000 in tax revenue in the same year from income and admission taxes, while the city government received approximately $300,000 from sales taxes. In 2012, 598 refugees were resettled in the Cleveland area.[14]

The other big concern some people have about refugees has to do with jobs in America. Specifically, "Will refugees and immigrants take my job?" Some Americans assume that immigrants and refugees take the jobs that otherwise would be given to Americans. However, Daniel Griswold, director of the Center for Policy Studies at the Cato Institute, argues:

Immigrants do not push Americans out of jobs. . . . Immigrants tend to fill jobs that Americans cannot or will not fill, mostly at the high and low ends of the skill spectrum. Immigrants are disproportionately represented in such high-skilled fields as medicine, physics, and computer science, but also in the lower-skilled sector such as hotels, restaurants, domestic service, construction, and light manufacturing.[15]

Neither do immigrants rely on public and government financial support to care for their families. In 2010, only 1 percent of the Supplemental Nutrition Assistance Program, formerly known as food stamp, users were refugees, and 99 percent of the SNAP users were not refugees. These facts can be used as part of the formation of Christians to provide a more accurate picture of who refugees are and what role they play in American society. It is another unfortunate reality that the reputation and truth about refugees and immigrants seldom align.

On socioeconomic issues, we see how fear of being in need can cause people to respond with harsh, irrational, and unjustifiable judgments against refugees and immigrants. But what is the Christian's response? Shouldn't they rely on the trustworthiness of God's promises? Of course, but that can be far easier said than done—unless the Christian embraces the character of God. After all, "My God shall supply all of your needs by his riches in glory by Christ Jesus" (Philippians 4:19 ESV). God's storehouse is indescribably more than enough to provide for refugees and immigrants while providing not only for you but supplying you and other Christians with the sufficiency to help meet the needs of neighbors. It can be a simple but profound matter of how we view God. Do we see our God as a God who provides in scarcity or abundance? Our perspective will determine our response. Nevertheless, God has spoken.

> "So do not worry, saying, 'What shall we eat?' or 'What shall we drink?' or 'What shall we wear?' For the pagans run after all these things, and your heavenly Father knows

that you need them. But seek first his kingdom and his righteousness, and all these things will be given to you as well." (Matthew 6:31–33 NIV)

Our refugee families at Gateway of Grace Ministries are some of hardest-working people I have ever known. One volunteer, after knowing a few refugee families, shared with me:

> My respect for refugees and immigrants has grown by leaps and bounds. I see them as very courageous to leave their culture, their extended families and friends, reputations and places of honor within their communities to come here to make a new, and hopefully better, and safer life for their families. Most are humble enough, and brave enough, to do what they must in terms of work to support their families. There are women who have never worked outside their homes (some who are illiterate) taking on jobs (often in hijabs and chadors) *with pride* to help support their families. There are professional individuals of both genders who will work at menial jobs for as long as it takes for them to get the credentials in their field to resume their careers as doctors, lawyers, engineers, bankers.

There is another question that I am certain to get before a speaking event is over: "Can refugees become independent and succeed on their own?" The success of refugees requires what the report from the Refugee Council of Australia calls "ingredients for success" that include, "having had community support; feeling motivated to 'give back' to society; and having access to training, English classes, mentoring, cultural, sporting, and volunteering activities."[16]

These are some of the elements that by loving our neighbor, we can play an essential role in providing. It is a blessing for us to be used by God to give new hope to people and to be a part of refugees' and immigrants' life stories as they will tell of them decades from now to their children and grandchildren. Do you want to be a part of God's story of hope, redemption, and success for their lives?

Other concerns voiced by some Americans include whether immigrants and refugees choose to integrate into our culture, and how their culture changes ours. It is important to know the difference between integration and assimilation. In his book, *Immigrants of the Kingdom of God*, Annang Asumang identifies the latter as a harmful view that demands abandoning one's identity and taking on the identity of their newly adopted country.[17] Assimilation is becoming completely like the culture around us. Integration, on the other hand, has to do with taking on what is good, lawful, and necessary for flourishing, productivity, relationship-building, and success in the new culture and, at the same time, keeping what is good and valuable about the former culture. The concerns for integration are not new. Griswold conveys, "In the mid-1800s, Irish immigrants were scored as lazy drunks, not to mention Roman Catholics. At the turn of the century a wave of 'new immigrants'— Poles, Italians, Russian Jews—were believed to be too different to ever assimilate into American life."[18]

It is true that immigrants and refugees change our culture. In Dallas, one can find restaurants, within a five-mile radius, from almost any continent. Ethnic grocery stores offer us not only options for healthy cooking, but also an adventurous experience. People from different races, nationalities, and languages bring our lives richness as we walk through the mall and hear different languages and see different ethnic attire. Refugees and immigrants also bring familial values that sometimes are lost in the United States, such as valuing the elderly, having a deeper respect for community, creating deeper connections with extended family, and so on. These are a few of the benefits of having refugees and immigrants in the United States.

They also set for us examples of courage and resilience. One of our volunteers describes a defining relationship for her as she loves these neighbors:

> I have a warm friendship with a highly educated family from Iraq. Watching this family embrace their new homeland with determination to be contributing Americans has been nothing short of amazing! They have all perfected their English, worked at building real and meaningful relationships with Americans, studied and became citizens, gone back to school in their respective professions to be licensed, and are teaching their next generation to value their new culture without forgetting the valuable traditions of their heritage.

Another volunteer shared this account of her relationship with a young Arab woman:

> I began the relationship with a young mother and her five children three years ago. The husband, who struggled with severe PTSD and holds a stronger commitment and sense of responsibility to his mother, abandoned his wife and children in Turkey while the family waited for refugee status to be granted in the United States This family of six arrived in the United States with clothing and two

blankets, no money, no English, and against the wishes
of her very conservative Muslim family. I have seen her
accept the help of churches and Christian organizations
to make a life in which she now supports for her family.
I have seen her struggle with the heartbreak and questions
of being let down by her religion. I see her willingly choosing the long, hard, but necessary path to a better life for
her children through learning the language and a commitment to education. She braves the death threats of
her family overseas and allows her children to continue
to thrive in a small Christian school because she values
the academic and character education they receive.

Asumang gives us qualities that are necessary for integration to take
place. Using Ruth as an example, he cites her "commitment, humil-
ity, hard work, and her willingness to be discipled and directed."[19]
Many refugees embrace these qualities, either naturally or out of
necessity. Either way, the Church can help. As Asumang suggests
in the biblical model of integration, "Ruth's successful integration
was a result of a combination of her own excellent personal qualities, the contribution of the community and God's grace." He says
that, "Without the receiving country providing the atmosphere of
welcome and friendly acceptance, the immigrant will not success-
fully integrate into their new environment."[20] An example of this
kind of failure is Samson in the Book of Judges. Asumang identifies
Samson's lack of knowledge of God as one of the reasons he failed.

The Church can help refugees in this area as well. When someone
has lost everything familiar to them, our compassion gives them a
sense of self-worth and confidence; when they lose their dignity
and are humiliated by their own government and its people and

are not welcomed by people in the new country, refugees and immigrants will strive to hold on to as much as possible of their cultural identity. Integration is much harder when they feel the best they can do is cling to what little they have as an identity. When we love them unconditionally as Christ loves us, we can build relationships with them to communicate that they are valued, loved, and accepted for who they are, regardless of possessions or socioeconomic status. This brings down the walls and gives them the freedom to embrace integration.

The Problem with Fear, Prejudices, and the Unknowing

The problem with both fear and prejudice is that they erode our souls and keep us from loving refugees, immigrants, the poor, and other marginalized groups. If we lose sight of who we are as neighbors, we cannot love God because the two go hand in hand. The proof of loving God is loving our neighbor. Prejudices are extremely destructive! If we are truly filled with the Spirit of God and obedient to the Bible, prejudices should cause extreme inner conflict in us. Prejudices should cause in our soul something similar to what food poisoning does to our bodies. Our Baptismal Covenant puts us on the right path from the outset. I love this covenant because it sums up beautifully how our faith in the Triune God and our walk in the teachings of the Apostles lead us to work for justice and truth. It also reclaims the dignity of every human being that is disregarded and at times destroyed by evil powers. This is a missional covenant. We are baptized to do God's work that is antithetical to prejudices.

Celebrant: Do you believe in God the Father?

People: I believe in God, the Father almighty, creator of heaven and earth.

Celebrant: Do you believe in Jesus Christ, the Son of God?

People: I believe in Jesus Christ, his only Son, our Lord. He was conceived by the power of the Holy Spirit and born of the Virgin Mary. He suffered under Pontius Pilate, was crucified, died, and was buried. He descended to the dead. On the third day he rose again. He ascended into heaven, and is seated at the right hand of the Father. He will come again to judge the living and the dead.

Celebrant: Do you believe in God the Holy Spirit?

People: I believe in the Holy Spirit, the holy catholic Church, the communion of saints, the forgiveness of sins, the resurrection of the body, and the life everlasting.

Celebrant: Will you continue in the apostles' teaching and fellowship, in the breaking of bread, and in the prayers?

People: I will, with God's help.

Celebrant: Will you persevere in resisting evil, and, whenever you fall into sin, repent and return to the Lord?

People: I will, with God's help.

Celebrant: Will you proclaim by word and example the Good News of God in Christ?

People: I will, with God's help.

Celebrant: Will you seek and serve Christ in all persons, loving your neighbor as yourself?

People: I will, with God's help.

Celebrant: Will you strive for justice and peace among all people, and respect the dignity of every human being?

People: I will, with God's help.

Do You See the Burning Bush?

During my visits to churches, I meet many people who have no strong feelings, either good or bad, about refugees, immigrants, or marginalized people. They recognize many of the conditions that force people to flee their homes and countries, and they are not afraid to have them in their neighborhoods. Yet for various reasons, they are not motivated in getting to know them. I suggest part of the issue is there has not been an encounter. I don't mean an introduction or a two-minute welcome to the neighborhood. I mean the kind of encounter in which the presence of God is indisputable, similar to the experience of Moses in Exodus 3.

Moses woke early one morning, probably expecting another typical day of tending his flock. He led it into the wilderness, like any other day, minding his own business, not looking for trouble or extra work. He already had a demanding job with a large extended family, with members who were "in his business" all the time, as families in the east were known for doing. If he lived today, his Google Calendar would be full.

Moses's very normal day suddenly turned very abnormal as we see from the scripture: "There the angel of the Lord appeared to him in a flame of fire out of a bush; he looked, and the bush was blazing, yet it was not consumed" (Exodus 3:2). And he says, "I must turn aside and look at this great sight, and see why the bush is not burned up" (Exodus 3:3). Moses is far more curious about the bush that doesn't burn up than he is about the angel. But what is important is that Moses paid attention. He could have continued with business as usual, but he chose to check out this unusual occurrence, and in so doing, God spoke to him. How many times in your life do you think God gives you a burning bush?

For many of us, the demands of our day keep us at a frantic pace. There is work or school, meetings, our kids' practice and games, the gym, preparing dinner, and on and on the list goes. To be fair, these are important tasks. However, we can be so overcommitted and just busy that it is hard for something unique or special to get our attention. Our fast-paced society makes our lives so noisy that it is very difficult to hear the voice of God—the thing that God desires to say specifically to you and me. Imagine an angel trying to get the attention of someone at the mall during the Christmas shopping season with all the lights, sounds, and attractions. Moses encountered God in the wilderness, a place of quiet and solitude. Moses was alone in the wilderness where no other voices were around.

I wrote this portion of the book during Lent. One of the purposes of observing Lent is for us to go into the wilderness, to be quiet and not only hear from God, but discern our demons. Remember, Jesus was tempted in the wilderness. In our wilderness, there can also be the routine duties and responsibilities of life. For Moses, being in the wilderness was another day on the job. He was not on a sabbatical at a mountain retreat center. Consider the various ways God revealed himself to Moses. God saved Moses through water, and later, God again made his awesome works known through the parting of the Red Sea. Here we are at Mount Horeb, which means parched or dry mountain, and Moses encounters God. We have preconceived ideas of how we will encounter God, and we look for them. Instead, God chooses to speak to us in unexpected ways and times and unusual places, like he did with Moses.

Yes, God absolutely speaks to us in the quiet solitude times of life. However, God is in no way limited to those situations. Therefore, it is important for us to develop our discernment so that we hear God's voice when he is speaking to us in unexpected places and through unfamiliar people.

Now, we arrive at these beautiful verses that explain why God revealed himself to Moses.

> Then the Lord said, "I have observed the misery of my people who are in Egypt; I have heard their cry on account of their taskmasters. Indeed, I know their sufferings, and I have come down to deliver them from the Egyptians . . . . So come, I will send you to Pharaoh to bring my people, the Israelites, out of Egypt." (Exodus 3:7–8, 10)

Obviously, I never met Moses, but I am certain that when he woke that day, he didn't have any expectations of a lunch meeting with an angel, and certainly not a plan to confront the Pharaoh.

A very common mistake we make as Christians is to equate religious activity with being a faithful Christian or living a Christian life. Or we seek to experience God and his presence as a measure of holiness. They are not. These are good in and of themselves, but if we stop there, we fall short of experiencing the fullness of life in Christ. We are called to center ourselves in Christ, worship God, receive Communion so that we go out and fulfill God's mission, not merely to feel happy or holy and energized to face our busy week.

Look at what God says to Moses: "I have observed the misery, heard the cry, known the suffering, and have come down to save. So, I send you, Moses." Let's look closer: "I have come down to save, so I send YOU!" The presence of God was to equip his prophet with a message. God had countless ways of saving his people and dealing with Pharaoh. But his purpose included turning this sheep herder into a shepherd for the Israelites. And we know of another shepherd. God came down in Jesus and brought salvation. Now, God sends you and me, in the power of the Spirit, with a message of freedom, hope, healing, and salvation in Christ. Jesus brings even greater clarity to our mission when he says, "as you did it to one of the least of these . . . you did it to me" (Matthew 25:40).

The scripture says Moses was afraid to look and see God. The beginning months of 2019 were bloody months for Christians in Nigeria. Hundreds of them were killed by Fulani Islamic extremists. In Iran, more than one hundred Christians are arrested every month. Then came the terror attacks in New Zealand carried out by a nationalist terrorist. We have seen recent natural disasters and plane crashes. Every day thousands of people are victims of human trafficking. If we are honest with ourselves, it is difficult and even scary to see the face of God in people who suffer.

We tend to pay attention for a little bit, maybe even say a prayer, and then we forget about them because their conditions and pain are just overwhelming. We also see and hear about so much suffering that we become desensitized. Once we stop feeling their pain, we lose the motivation to respond. As Christians, we must guard our hearts and minds against becoming numb to the pain of those who are suffering, especially when it is in our power to affect change in their circumstances. When we look into the faces of our suffering neighbors, regardless of their country of origin, race, or religious beliefs, we encounter God who commands us to reach out for Christ's sake.

Let me encourage you at this point not to lose heart. God has not called any one of us to fix all the problems of the world. However, God has equipped each of us to bring hope and salvation into many of these situations. Like Moses, you may be saying to yourself, "What can I do? I'm just one person. How can I have an impact on something as big as those problems?" God is saying to you and me the same words he said to Moses in his wilderness, "I will be with you" (Exodus 3:12). As Paul encouraged the saints at Philippi, "I can do all things through [Christ] who strengthens me" (Philippians 4:13 ESV). And "he who began a good work in you will carry it on to completion until the day of Christ Jesus" (Philippians 1:6 NIV).

Meditate on this truth: God never fails at what he promises. I believe there are three core points to embrace from the burning bush Moses experienced. First, pay attention to the ways God is calling you, in quiet and in busyness. Just like the bush that was not being consumed, God's calling for your life will not go away. By calling, I do not mean the big vocational decision, but loving your neighbors; individuals and situations that are in front of you and you learn about regularly.

Second, God calls each of us to love our neighbor. God's calling is not only for those in full-time ministry—and the Christian life is far more than coming to church, attending small groups, or even Bible study. God desires for each of us to move into the deep waters of our faith because his heart is for restoration, healing, hope, and salvation of all people.

Third, God's call will move us out of our comfort zones and many times bring us face to face with people of power and influence, who like Pharaoh are opposed to salvation and hope for the oppressed. If everything we do in Christ is easy and free of conflict, we may want to examine whether we have moved into the deep waters of our faith. As St. Paul shared with the Christians at Philippi, "For God is at work within you, helping you want to obey him, and then helping you do what he wants" (Philippians 2:13 TLB).

My Neighbor, Patriotism, Nationalism

Ideology: we all have one, whether we acknowledge it or are even aware of it. An ideology is a system of ideas and ideals, especially one that forms the basis of economic or political theory and policy or opinions. Do you know where you are, ideologically, or have you ever given serious thought to it? According to a Gallup poll of 2010, seventy-four percent of Americans describe themselves as either very or extremely patriotic.[21] According to another poll, political conservatives form the majority of the people in the United States, followed by moderates.[22]

Patriotism, which is a feeling of altruism and genuine love for the country, has become confused with nationalism. Nationalism is identification with one's own nation and support for its interests, especially to the exclusion or detriment of the interests of other nations. Patriotism is a good thing, and while nationalism may seem to share certain characteristics, it certainly does not hold the values of patriotism. Consider the nationalism of Nazi Germany and the misery it brought upon the world.

There are also more subtle ways that nationalism shows up—for example, the way many people in the United States responded to the Jewish refugees that we mentioned earlier. Or reflect on what you have heard from friends, family, church members, and news outlets about refugees and immigrants. Based on the cumulative information, would these people be more aligned with patriotism or nationalism? More importantly, could they live out their convictions and still be obedient followers of Christ?

Authentic Christianity does not fit into any political persuasions. As Tony Evans of Oak Cliff Bible Fellowship Church in Dallas and The Urban Alternative often says so wonderfully, "God does not ride on the backs of donkeys and elephants. And Jesus did not come to take sides, but to take over."

I was born and raised in an ancient country with a glorious history where Cyrus the Great was used by God to save the Israelites from Babylonian slavery. He also is credited with writing the first charter of human rights. From science to arts to engineering, the Persian Empire led the world for centuries. So, I can certainly identify with feeling pride in heritage and patriotism. I also hear it often in conversations with some Iranian-Americans when they speak of our heritage. It is good to remember and be proud of the great contributions of a culture or nation. But, that national pride and honor of heritage can subtly and quickly become idolatry if they are given a place in our hearts that is superior to our identity in Christ.

Further, if we see ourselves as superior to others who are also created in God's image, given the breath of life by God, and for whom Christ died on the cross, we deceive ourselves and defame the character of Christ. Each of us has a need to belong and a desire to connect with our earthly origins. Sometimes, those needs of belonging and national identity lead to paths that God never intended. The ways in which we search to fill those longings of the heart remind me of Johnny Lee's 1980 song about looking for love in all the wrong places.

As those who have been born again from above, we have a new heritage, a new hope, and a new identity. We are part of a new nation, not built with human hands, and with a birthright beyond this world's comprehension. I suggest that now more than ever, we should surrender to God's desire for us to think and live above any heritages, temporal titles, and boundaries to embrace our supreme position granted to us through the cross of Christ. That is when neighbors from any region of the world will experience his Spirit within us.

We the Church

One of the most admired documents in history and certainly in this nation begins with the words, "We the People." In the Preamble, the framers of the Constitution of the United States set forth the vision to create "a more perfect Union, establish Justice, insure domestic Tranquility, provide for the common defense, promote the general Welfare, and secure the Blessings of Liberty" for themselves and for generations to come.

As the Church was being established, the early framers of Christianity had similar questions: Who are we? What is our purpose?

Why do we exist? They wanted to make the statement, *We the Church*. Fortunately for them, history was on their side. They could look back into the Old Testament and know the character of God and God's purposes. What God did in choosing Israel to be the People of God provided the early Church and us with a forecast of where God was leading. Let's look at Isaiah 49:6 (NIV):

> "It is too small a thing for you to be my servant to restore the tribes of Jacob and bring back those of Israel I have kept. I will also make you a light for the Gentiles, that my salvation may reach to the ends of the earth."

God chose the Israelites as God's People. God did not choose them because he loved them exclusively, but so that they would be a light to the nations. God says that to save only the tribes of Israel is too small for his love. God chose Israel in order that all the peoples of the earth may be healed. The universal nature of God's mission for his people did not stop with his choosing of Israel. It was always intended to become the mission of the Church in the New Testament. Just as Israel was not chosen to be a self-serving people for the sake of their own pleasure and purposes, the Church is not to be a self-serving exclusive club for socialization and group therapy. The Church exists for the sake of the world because God wants healing for all nations, our neighbors near and far! God's healing is for those we love, those we don't, those we have known and those we will never know, those on your street and those in Syria and sub-Saharan Africa.

The Church's main mission is the healing of the nations to the ends of the earth through the gospel. Acts 8:26–40, the story of the Ethiopian eunuch, adds a hopeful and inclusive account regarding the availability of the gospel to all. Likewise, on the day of Pentecost, God made explicit this desire and gave power to the disciples to reach all peoples with the gospel. Later, Paul became the apostle to the Gentiles and even suffered much tribulation for the sake of sharing the gospel with them.[23] The New Testament is filled with hope for those who do not know God and have not received God's healing. This hope is to be carried out by the Church as Jesus commissioned his disciples. He is still commissioning us! Are you ready?

> "Go therefore and make disciples of all nations, baptizing them in the name of the Father and of the Son and of the Holy Spirit." (Matthew 28:19)

Disciple-making is the same today as it was two thousand years ago. People need to know and receive the Gospel of Jesus Christ. This Good News is not an intellectual proposition or a platform for religious debate; neither is it the possession of an elite group to hold it over others with a sense of moral superiority. The Gospel of Jesus Christ is the real, sacrificial, incarnate love of God poured into the world to change our hopelessness into hope and heal our infected wounds of injustice, hatred, division, and idolatry. The Good News of Jesus Christ is a reality that brings healing and reconciliation into the lives of those who put their trust in Jesus.[24]

Along with eternal life, the gospel also brings healing in this life. It is so much more than gaining heaven when we die. The Kingdom of God is not a euphoric experience based on another world, but an irrevocable promise that transforms the physical as well as the spiritual. This Good News carries us as we struggle to love our enemies and bless those who persecute us. It moves us to share a meal with people unlike us for the chance to reveal Christ's love to them. Are you ready?

Regarding the mission of the Church, N.T. Wright states, "[It] must reflect and be shaped by the future hope as the New Testament presents it."[25] In light of the resurrection of Jesus Christ, Wright reflects on the mission of the Church in three areas: justice, beauty, and evangelism. Wright shares, "Part of the task of the Church must be to take up that sense of injustice, to bring it to speech, to help people articulate it and, when they are ready to do so, to turn it into prayer."[26] It is through prayer that the Church is stirred by the Spirit into action in order to foster healing and reconciliation at every level, social and personal, physical and spiritual.

Regarding the beauty of creation, Revelation 21:1 offers an incredible image of the future that God has for his creation. The verses reveal God's glorious plans for "the new heaven and the new earth." God will not dispose of the physical world. Caring for the earth and restoring its beauty—it is so much more than being merely an environmentalist. It involves ". . . the message of a new creation, of the beauty of the present world taken up and transcended in the beauty of the world that is to be—with part of that beauty being precisely the healing of the present anguish."[27] Concerning evangelism, the mission of the Church is not about sharing information regarding the person of Jesus Christ. It implores everyone and anyone to receive the forgiveness of sin, reconciliation, and healing by helping them awake from darkness and to choose to live in the light of Jesus Christ.

The work of justice and caring for the beauty of creation reaches completion by healing the emotional and spiritual wounds of the people and their reconciliation into friendship with God.

Friendship with God takes place in and through the Holy Spirit who indwells the person and community. While the Holy Spirit is at work in the world, even among those who do not know the hope of Christ, being indwelt by the Spirit and thus having friendship with God is a promise of Jesus to those who follow him and put their trust in him. The indwelling of the Holy Spirit is fully related to the mission of the Church as we see on the day of Pentecost. In Acts 2:11, Arabs, Medes, and others hear the spoken words by the apostles as the declaration of "the wonders of God in our own tongues" (NIV).

Before we can love our neighbor, we must be in fellowship with the Spirit through prayer. Loving our neighbor is directly related to our willingness to surrender to the Holy Spirit's presence and work. Without fellowship with the Spirit and friendship with the Father, you and I can be easily blinded to our neighbors. You and I are the physical presence in the world through which the Holy Spirit fulfills the purposes of God.

Our Heritage

A few years ago, my husband gave me an ancestry kit as one of my Christmas gifts. I was so excited, but also a little nervous to learn about all the people who have contributed in some way to who I am. It turned out to be one of the biggest blessings of my life. There was some information that I knew from my parents and grandparents, and some that I had suspected based on a bit of geographical information. Then there was DNA evidence that not only surprised me, but also gave me a greater sense of pride. There is something special about knowing that you are connected to a much broader family that you never met and to peoples who did significant things with their life. Like all family trees, I am sure there were those who did not shine their brightest in my lineage.

When we look into scripture, we get glimpses of our Christian heritage. And, like tracing my heritage through an ancestry kit, we get to celebrate some heroes in the family and learn from the failures of others. It is the same for the Church today. We are one humongous family spanning the globe and centuries. And despite the flaws and accomplishments throughout these vast spiritual relationships, we are family because God, in grace, chose to pour love into each of us so that God's healing can reach the world. What a privilege. As we carry on the family heritage of faith, we do so under the same family name—Christian. It is my mission and yours, and everyone's who has placed his or her faith in Jesus Christ. It is ours because we have been placed in our Father's mission, the Church. Fulfilling that mission means we are connected to a plan he gave to our spiritual ancestors thousands of years ago, to love our neighbor so that they may know God's love.

We also see that failing to carry on God's mission came with a warning for the People of God. Look at what it says in Isaiah 1:17–23): "Learn to do good; Seek justice, Reprove the ruthless; Defend the orphan, Plead for the widow" (v. 17 NAS). He continues, "Come now, and let us reason together" (v. 18 NAS). He then shares the nature of the transgression of the People: ". . . They do not bring justice to the fatherless, and the widow's cause does not come to them" (v. 23 ESV).

Loving our neighbor is not a special calling for the spiritually mature. As a member in the family of God, it is part of carrying on our heritage handed down through the ages. Paul reflects on this matter in 1 Corinthians 12 by identifying the Church as the

Body of Christ. Each member has a gift for the purpose of gospel ministry. Each member is needed for the wholeness of the body and for accomplishment of its tasks. He explains the variety of services and activities that are empowered by God (v. 4–5). According to Paul, each Christian has a gift that was given with the expectation that it would enrich the Body as it carries on the work. No member is useless to the cause of Christ or excluded from the responsibility of making him known. Each Christian has the Holy Spirit living within to empower and guide not only the individual, but collectively to multiply the Church until the whole world hears the gospel.

1 Peter 2:9 (NIV) offers another aspect of the ministry of God's people: "But you are a chosen people, a royal priesthood, a holy nation, God's special possession, that you may declare the praises of him who called you out of darkness into his wonderful light." As Israel was set apart by God to live a heritage to the glory of God, so the Church is set apart, not for her own sake, but to declare the praises of God, providing witnesses to God's mighty power of salvation through Jesus Christ. Are you ready to be an instrument that can help your neighbor come to praise the Lord through your demonstration of faithful love in action and word?

If you are like most Christians, the term "royal priesthood" is not one that rolls smoothly off the lips. But it is one of the identifying positions we hold in the Kingdom of God. In the Old Testament, the priest would intercede on behalf of the people and return to the people with a blessing from God. One of the most important ministries of God's people is to be a priesthood, making intercessions on behalf of others. How often do you intercede on behalf of your atheist, Jewish, Hindu, and Muslim neighbors?

Matthew 5:13–14 offers beautiful imagery of the People of God as the "city built on a hill," "the salt of the earth," and "the light of the world." These are not glorifying attributes of an institution for hymns on Sunday mornings. These attributes are given as a commissioning for Kingdom work to the nations. The Book of Common Prayer summarizes the ministry of all God's People: "The ministry of lay persons is to represent Christ and his Church; to bear witness to him wherever they may be; and, according to the gifts given them, to carry on Christ's work of reconciliation in the world; and to take their place in the life, worship, and governance of the Church."[28] What gifts do you have with which to love and bless your neighbor?

As Teresa of Avila beautifully put it, "Christ has no body but yours, no hands, no feet on earth but yours, yours are the eyes with which he looks with compassion on this world."[29] The ministry of all People of God is to be the hands and feet of Christ in the world.[30] The heritage of the People of God is to look with compassion on the broken world and people who are oppressed by sin and injustice, both physical and spiritual. It is to allow our eyes to be the eyes of Jesus by the power of the Holy Spirit. In the gospel we read, "When he saw the crowds, he had compassion on them, because they were harassed and helpless, like sheep without a shepherd" (Matthew 9:36 NIV).

Balancing Obedience?

The truth about obedience is many Christians would be perfectly okay if the subject never came up in conversation or a sermon. For many, the term evokes thoughts of controlling, oppressive, and manipulative preachers who are notoriously unskilled in the scripture and are legalistic. But when it comes to loving our neighbor, obeying the voice of God frees us from cultural and prejudicial chains. We know God's command to love our neighbor; the poor, the stranger, the oppressed, the refugee, the orphan, and the widow, and yet it is hard for us to love. There is an internal conflict or lack of integration between us and the demands of the Kingdom of God. As Paul says, "For I do not do the good I want to do, but the evil I do not want to do—this I keep on doing" (Romans 7:19 NIV). As we see from this verse, most often we do our own will, rather than God's. Obedience helps us integrate what we know and how we live. We belong to Christ and obedience creates the discipline in us to behave like Christians, and through that, God transforms us and heals our wounds of prejudices and fears.

Paul says, "Do not conform to the pattern of this world, but be transformed by the renewing of your mind. Then you will be able to test and approve what God's will is—his good, pleasing and perfect will" (Romans 12:2). Renewing our minds happens by the power of the Holy Spirit as we obey his commandment to love our neighbor. Another way of saying it is, "Trust in the LORD with all your heart and lean not on your own understanding; in all your ways submit to him, and he will make your paths straight" (Proverbs 3:5–6).

Concerning how we view our refugee and immigrant neighbors and how we view ourselves in relationship to them, let's see what is in line with the scripture and the witness of the Church. Augustine, for example, argued that the Christian should see themselves as a pilgrim passing through. He said that we are not citizens of an earthly kingdom, but rather citizens of the city of God.[31] To prove this same point, scholar Miroslav Volf in his book, *Exclusion and*

Embrace, also used the example of Paul, saying that he "insisted on the religious irrelevance of genealogical ties and on the sole sufficiency of faith. His horizon was the whole world, and he himself was traveling missionary, proclaiming the Good News of Jesus Christ—the seed of Abraham who fulfilled God's promise that through Abraham 'all the nations will be blessed' (Galatians 3:8)."[32]

I started Gateway of Grace Ministries as a missionary. The staff consisted of me, myself, and I. Because I was still trying to recruit volunteers, I did everything from collecting furnishings and housewares and baby items, to moving furniture for new refugee families, to taking them to appointments, and helping enroll their children in school and doing translations for various services. During that time, I met an amazing woman of God. She was a prayerful person with a servant's heart as big as Texas. She had a ranch in west Texas, wore cowboy boots, and had a really big pickup. She was a prickly-pear-picking and target-shooting Texas gal. But she grew up in a family with a lifestyle that was far different than what she would become. Her family was the kind that used proper china settings and sterling silver at every meal. Before getting involved with Gateway of Grace, she had trepidation about immigrants and refugees because she never had a relationship with them. Everything believed about them was formed completely on what she learned from media. She also had a few strong political views about them, simply because she did not know any refugees.

She had been restless, searching for God's calling for her life a few months prior to our meeting. She had been wrestling with Romans 10:14–15 (NIV):

> How, then, can they call on the one they have not believed
> in? And how can they believe in the one of whom they

have not heard? And how can they hear without someone preaching to them? And how can anyone preach unless they are sent? As it is written: "How beautiful are the feet of those who bring good news."

Next, she met me and found out about a refugee who was in need of a sofa. She donated one. Her church was a partner church with Gateway of Grace, and they adopted a refugee family from Iraq. She became involved. She was scared, but seeing others serving refugees helped her to step into something that was completely outside of her purview, something that was initially extremely uncomfortable. Serving "foreign people," as she puts it, was not something she had ever done. But in obedience to this prompting of the Holy Spirit, she put her faith into action. She believes that God taught her how to love the stranger and to face the fear of the unknowing. She soon realized that refugees were just people. Obedience to love these strangers gave her a deep appreciation for what they had gone through and the hard work they were putting into starting a new life in the United States She says that being loved in such deep ways by Christians was shocking to the family she served. The refugee family soon realized the difference between Christians and others because of the unconditional love. She knew God's command to love "the stranger" and what God had asked her to do, but she never understood what it really meant and how deep and transformative it was until she actually obeyed it. Obedience changed her heart toward refugees, and helped her become stronger in her faith.

Today my friend faithfully serves, and God is still calling her to the deeper ways of loving and serving. She fell in love with a large family that consisted of a few brothers and their families. She started loving them, serving them, taking them on mission trips with her church, and having Christmas dinners with them. The youngest of the brothers, who is in his twenties, moved to Houston. He became ill and my friend drove from Dallas to Houston, a four-hour drive, to take him to the doctor because she was worried about him. Who does that but someone who has been transformed by the power of the Holy Spirit to love their neighbor?

Obedience in loving our neighbor also brings God's world closer to us and makes the suffering of all people for whom Christ has died more real to us. A Gateway of Grace volunteer describes it in this way:

> Before I began working with refugees, their plight was remote and abstract to me. I could disconnect myself from it and look at their stories as something that happens to "them," not to us. That makes it easy to distance oneself emotionally from the pain that someone else is going through, which is what, in my privilege, I unintentionally did. There is no way to disconnect that way anymore. It is impossible to listen to their stories—from them, not from the news—and ever go back to seeing their problems as distant. Seeing the fear, pain, and exhaustion in a mother's eyes is haunting.

Ministry of Reconciliation

So from now on we regard no one from a worldly point of view. Though we once regarded Christ in this way, we do so no longer. Therefore, if anyone is in Christ, the new creation has come: The old has gone, the new is here! All this is from God, who reconciled us to himself through

Christ and gave us the ministry of reconciliation: that God was reconciling the world to himself in Christ, not counting people's sins against them. And he has committed to us the message of reconciliation. (2 Corinthians 5:16–19)

The traditional pattern of missions and evangelism has been sending missionaries to other countries to fulfill the Great Commission and share Christ's love in practical ways with the world. It seems, however, that God is bringing more of the nations to us. Refugees are coming to us. It would be extremely dangerous and costly to send missionaries across Africa, Asia, and the Middle East. While the patterns of migration and refugee resettlement can be explained factually using social and political sciences, we must look above and beyond and seek God's hand at work even in the midst of the tragedies and brokenness of the world.

At the inauguration of the Temple in Jerusalem, in 2 Chronicles 2:32–33, Solomon prayed a beautiful prayer. It reminds us that, even while we work to meet the many pressing needs of foreigners, refugees, and immigrants, the heart of God's will is that they may know the name of the Lord. Where does this fall in the discussion of loving our neighbor? A few years ago, after finishing their annual service project with Gateway of Grace, students from a partner Episcopal church were greeted with a beautiful spread by our adult English as a Second Language students. The students were mostly Muslim from different countries, and the food was absolutely generous and beautiful. A new student who was a very strict Muslim woman from Somalia was with us. Her English was very limited. I invited her several times to join us and take part in the beautiful feast but she wouldn't. She and her children seemed to be hungry but she had a fearful look on her face. Finally, she asked me if that was "religious" food. I was confused at first. I told her that it was not and we had religious food only at church: the Lord's Supper. Eventually, she was able to communicate that she was afraid that God would strike her or her children dead if she ate of our food because we were Christian and thus unclean. Her fear and concerns were real. My heart was broken for her and my compassion deep. Can you imagine living your life in constant fear that you would do something that is against God's commandments and God would strike you or punish your family? I asked myself what it would look like to love (agape) that woman. What did God want for her to know? What kind of relationship God would want with her? The passage from 2 Chronicles became very real because it was very clear that the woman did not know the name of the Lord as Love. She did not know that she was so deeply loved by God and God would not strike her or her children because they ate food with Christians.

A Gateway of Grace volunteer reflects on her experience of loving refugee neighbors:

> Being involved in the lives of refugees in a long-term, holistic ministry has given me a deeper understanding of finding Jesus in my journey, rather than a sprint to the finish line. Being able to walk with folks at various places on their journey to the Cross, I have come to understand that we don't know where we are intersecting someone's journey—at the beginning, somewhere in the middle, at the point of surrender, or beyond. It is vital that we are faithful in our own walk so that we can be a compass for those God brings into our lives.

Loving our neighbor is not just about them. It is about us. As the great theologian Hans Urs von Balthasar, in *A Theology of History*, reminds us, "The Christian and the Church attain to their true essence, their *eidos*, which exists already in Christ the Bridegroom, insofar as they receive and keep in themselves the will of the Father."[33] He describes the nature of mutuality in missions as he talks about the will of God as "the seed of grace, which is always both the seed of mission and, for that very reason, at the same time a seed of formation and development."[34] Loving our refugee and immigrant neighbors is this understanding of God's mission; a mutual relationship of healing and reconciliation made possible by the seed of God's grace.

While working on behalf of Christ for reconciliation, we must have a biblical understanding of what it entails, not a secular one. All secular understandings of the issue will leave us in despair. Three aspects of reconciliation are significant as Miroslav Volf describes them:

> First, the final reconciliation is not a work of human beings but of the triune God. Second, it is not an apocalyptic end of the world but the eschatological new beginning of this world. Third, the final reconciliation is not a self-enclosed "totality" because it rests on a God who is not [an intellectual] notion but a perfect love.[35]

Presently, many refugees come from Muslim countries. In light of the increased negative emotions toward Muslims in the United States, helping the Church understand a non-totalitarian way of reconciliation is a major task. It is paradoxical to work toward something that we know ultimately will not be completed by us and we must not expect it to be so, but that is what we are called to.

Volf offers a "non-final reconciliation" concept, which is a belief that I have adopted as the direction of this book: the concept that we participate in the mission of God the Holy Spirit until its fulfillment at *Parousia* or the Second Coming of Christ. The goal of participation in God's mission is not success, since there will always be the gulf between ideal and real. The goal, rather, is faithfulness in light of possible ways of loving our neighbors and the work of the Holy Spirit who also is already at work in the lives of refugees and immigrants in the United States. "The act of corresponding to what God wills for the world history—which is something given by grace but nevertheless put into effect by humanity—is the central core which makes history happen"[36] and which makes God's grace known to the world. The task therefore is equipping the saints for the work of ministry, as Ephesians 4:12 puts it.

We are not called to fulfill the Kingdom but participate in it. In his *Prophetic Imagination*, theologian Walter Brueggemann offers three actions that I believe will be helpful for framing loving our neighbors and moving Christians forward in light of this knowledge. First, there should be an "offering of symbols that are adequate to contradict a situation of hopelessness in which newness is unthinkable."[37] Second, we are "to bring to public expression those very hopes and yearnings that have been denied so long and suppressed so deeply that we no longer know they are there."[38] Third, we are to "speak metaphorically about hope but concretely about the real newness that comes to us and redefines our situation."[39]

These are very exciting, simple, and actionable frameworks. I have found that testimonies and stories of transformation, of both volunteers and refugees, can function in all three aspects of prophetic actions. In fact, all relational ministries fall into these frameworks and they can change our faith walk and move us, in the words of Maximus the Confessor, from merely "being" into the kind of "well-being" that is in line with "eternal being" and God's final destiny for the creation.[40] I believe that, regardless of political or denominational persuasion, even the hardest hearts can be transformed by the Holy Spirit. Many times, I have seen hard-hearted individuals transformed into loving neighbors to refugees. I have seen Sauls transformed into Pauls. We must be intentional about providing ways that open doors for the work of the Holy Spirit within us and the Church.

Our Common Humanity

Even in her late fifties, she was still beautiful. She carried herself gracefully, and her mannerisms reflected a traditional upbringing. As she started sharing her story, I sensed something strange about her. She had a sort of hopelessness and dark resignation in her countenance. She had been a part of the royal family in Afghanistan when the country was seized by the Soviet Union in the 1970s. The Russians killed all the male members of her family, including her father, brothers, and brother-in-law. They raped her, her mom, and her sister. The three women escaped and eventually became refugees in the United States. Her mom and sister, who had lost their husbands, never remarried, and she, who had been raped at a very young age and witnessed the murder of her family, never married.

As she was telling this horrendous story, her words were void of any emotion. The passage that kept coming to my mind was Isaiah

42:3, which says, "A bruised reed he will not break, and a dimly burning wick he shall not quench; he will faithfully bring forth justice." This woman was the bruised reed that had never met the Messiah, the one who had never received justice and healing. Her light burned dimly in hopelessness trapped in that childhood tragedy. As best as I could tell, no one had ever shared the healing love of Christ with her, even though she had lived in the United States for over twenty years. What a shame.

Her story stood in stark contrast with my own story. After coming to the United States and applying for asylum, on the first day of our arrival in Dallas, God connected us with a Baptist church through the ministry of an unlikely person who invited us to church. I was baptized there six months after our first visit. The ministry of that church to a Middle Eastern family that looked nothing like them was incredible. With the help and support of the church, we started building a new life of faith. When God called me to start Gateway of Grace, and as my husband and I were praying for a name to give this new ministry, I remembered what my Baptist church had done for us and how its ministry had changed my life. The church's seemingly unending flow of grace toward us stood out to me, and I was reminded of the truth that the main difference between Christianity and other religions was God's grace made tangible and experiential in the world through God's people. We knew the Church, as the instrument of God in the world, was the gateway of God's grace. We chose the name Gateway of Grace because it reflected the nature of the Christian ministry my family and I experienced from the Baptist church.

I cannot imagine what turns the course of my life would have taken without that church. Perhaps my life would have been wasted in hopelessness like the Afghan woman. Perhaps God would have used another church to reach us. Regardless, the faithfulness of that Baptist church, the Christian community, and the Body of Christ transformed our lives. I am forever grateful to God!

Practical Implications of Loving Our Neighbor

Jessica Stern, in her book *Terror in the Name of God*, interviewed terrorists from all three Abrahamic faiths. One of the issues that she addressed was how terrorists recruited members. Her findings confirmed commonalities with how gangs recruit.[41] Similarities between how gangs recruited and how terrorists recruited included targeting those not connected to a community, pursuing those who were socially or economically vulnerable, and finding those who did not have goals or a strong sense of self-worth and identity.[42] In other words, terrorists recruit individuals who feel powerless and invisible, or who live in cultures with radically different values.

Invisibility means "not being comprehended" in deep and significant ways, or in other words, not having meaningful and community relationships.[43] As mentioned earlier, refugees and immigrants struggle with issues of identity. Scholar Charles Taylor points out that, "Non-recognition or misrecognition can inflict harm, can be a form of oppression, imprisoning someone in a false, distorted, and reduced mode of being."[44] This can be a major point of vulnerability for refugees as they perceive the ways in which Americans view them and how they feel about them. As Christians, what kind of impact do we want to have on refugees and immigrants?

If terrorists or gang leaders understand how to use and feed the needs of the vulnerable people to further their agenda, how much more the Church should understand this. Real meaning, hope, friendship, and support can be provided to refugees by Christians. Our vulnerable neighbors are deeply in need of generosity and hospitality that are markers of Christian community. These elements of love are demands of reason, even if the refugee situation was looked at merely from a secular perspective. If we are not faithful to our vocation, it is more likely that unsavory groups, who recruit more effectively, will reach our neighbors. Eventually, as Stern confirms, the refugee and immigrant can be left vulnerable to be entrapped by radicalism.

Conclusion

We love our neighbors because it is an overflow of God's love for us through the Holy Spirit. We love refugees, immigrants, and all other marginalized people out of God's abundance through Christ. The Greek word that is used in John 10:10 to describe the kind of life Christ gives us is περισσὸν (*perisoss*), which means excessively or greater. We will always have more than enough so we can love and serve as God has purposed. There is no shortage with God. The God who creates all people also provides the resources to sustain them. Loving our neighbors helps us communicate and celebrate the reality of an abundant life through Christ and his victory over destructive and oppressive powers. It also celebrates God's creative genius in diversity of races. Through you and your love, Christ's words and works are revealed in real and tangible ways to those who don't know him.

It is a privilege to be used by God to love our neighbors and to make Christ's presence known to them. It is not a burden. And while God has called you and me to participate in his mission of restoration, healing, and salvation, it is our decision to respond properly. God will not force us to love and serve the poor, the stranger, the oppressed, the orphan, the widow, and the prisoner. He will, however, accomplish his purposes, with or without us. God always uses faithful people who are ready to serve. The question before us is whether we choose to say yes to God and be a part of his work. All of us need Christ's love and grace, and that certainly includes our neighbors. Jesus says, "I have other sheep that are not of this sheep pen. I must bring them also. They too will listen to my voice, and there shall be one flock and one shepherd" (John 10:16 NIV). How do you plan to be the hands, feet, and voice of Christ to your neighbor?

Notes

1 http://www.vatican.va/archive/ccc_css/archive/catechism/p3s1c1a5.htm

2 https://www.cdc.gov/heartdisease/facts.htm

3 Ashley Ross, "Why a History Lesson about World War II Refugees Went Viral," Time, November 18, 2015, accessed February 10, 2016, http://time.com/4118178/paris-attacks-jews-syrian-refugees-history/.

4 https://www.ushmm.org/research/about-the-mandel-center/initiatives /ethics-religion-holocaust/articles-and-resources/jews-and-christians-the-unfolding-interfaith-relationship

5 The Nicene Creed

6 "The Definition of Sin," accessed 03/10/19, http://www.vatican.va/archive/ENG0015/_P6A.HTM.

7 Ched Myers and Matthew Colwell, Our God Is Undocumented: Biblical Faith and Immigrant Justice (Maryknoll, NY: Orbis Books, 2012), 18.

8 Neil Patel and Pragya Kakani, "Do Americans Fear Muslims?", Harvard Political Review, February 13, 2014, http://harvardpolitics.com/united-states/do-americans-ear-muslims/.

9 Ibid.

10 "Statistics and Facts on the United States Advertising Industry," accessed 9/9/19, https://www.statista.com/topics/979/advertising-in-the-us/.

11 Ibid.

12 "Media Influence: Public Policy and Public Opinion," a speech to "Symposium II" at Nichols College, MA, November 4, 1982, accessed 9/9/19, https://department.monm.edu/cata/McGaan/Classes/INTG415/Paletz.pdf.

13 https://www.aph.gov.au/Parliamentary_Business/Committees/House_of_Representatives_Committees?url=mig/multiculturalism/report/chapter10.htm

14 Chmura Economics & Analytics, Economic Impact of Refugees in the Cleveland Area (Refugee Services of Collaborative of Greater Cleveland, 2013), accessed February 10, 2016, http://rsccleveland.org/wp-content/uploads/2013/10/ClevelandRefugeeEconomic-Impact.pdf.

15 Daniel Griswold, "Immigrants Have Enriched American Culture and Enhanced Our Influence in the World," Insight, February 18, 2002, accessed February 10, 2016, http://www.cato.org/publications/commentary/immigrants-have-enriched-american-culture-enhanced-our-influence-world.

16 Chmura Economics & Analytics, Economic Impact . . . .

17 Annang Asumang, *Immigrants of the Kingdom of God: Reflections on Immigration as a Metaphor of Christian Discipleship* (Eugene, OR: Wipf & Stock, 2008), 71.

18 Griswold, "Immigrants . . . ."

19 Asumang, *Immigrants of the Kingdom of God*, 63.

20 Ibid 73

21 Lymari Morales, "One in Three Americans 'Extremely Patriotic'," Gallup, July 2, 2010, accessed February 10, 2016, http://www.gallup.com/poll/141110/One-Three-Americans-Extremely-Patriotic.aspx.

22 Lydia Saad, "'Conservatives' Are Single-Largest Ideological Group," Gallup, June 15, 2009, accessed February 10, 2016, http://www.gallup.com/poll/120857/Conservatives-Single-Largest-Ideological-Group.aspx.

23 Ephesians 3.

24 Healing and reconciliation have been defined in the Central Theological Statement.

25 N.T. Wright, *Surprised by Hope: Rethinking Heaven, the Resurrection, and the Mission of the Church* (New York: HarperOne, 2008), 230.

26 Ibid., 231.

27 Ibid., 232.

28 "Catechism," 1979 Book of Common Prayer.

29 St. Teresa of Avila, "Journey with Jesus," accessed June 24, 2014, http://www.journeywithjesus.net/PoemsAndPrayers/Teresa_Of_Avila_Christ_Has_No_Body.shtml.

30 The details of this will be explained in the Ministry of Reconciliation section below.

31 St. Augustine, *The City of God* (426 ce).

32 Miroslav Volf, *Exclusion and Embrace: A Theological Exploration of Identity, Otherness, and Reconciliation* (Nashville: Abingdon Press, 1996), 43.

33 Hans Urs von Balthasar, *A Theology of History* (San Francisco: Ignatius Press, 1994), 123.

34 Ibid.

35 Volf, *Exclusion and Embrace*, 110.

36 von Balthasar, *A Theology of History*, 123.

37 Walter Brueggemann, *The Prophetic Imagination*, 2nd ed. (Minneapolis, MN: Fortress Press, 2001), 64.

38 Ibid.

39 Ibid.

40 Andrew Louth, *Maximus the Confessor* (London: Routledge, 1996), 103.

41 "Gangs and Your Child," National Crime Prevention Council, accessed February 10, 2016, http://archive.ncpc.org/topics/by-audience/parents/gangs-and-your-child.html.

42 Jessica Stern, *Terror in the Name of God "Why Religious Militants Kill"* (New York: HarperAudio, 2004).

43 Elizabeth Conde-Frazier, S. Steve Kang, and Gary A. Parrett, *A Many Colored Kingdom: Multicultural Dynamics for Spiritual Formation* (Grand Rapids, MI: Baker Academic, 2004), 71.

44 Charles Taylor, *Multiculturalism: Examining the Politics of Recognition* (Princeton, NJ: Princeton University Press, 1994), 25.

Printed in the USA
CPSIA information can be obtained
at www.ICGtesting.com
JSHW012056140824
68134JS00035B/3472